PRAY WITH FIRE

Guy Chevreau served the Baptist church from 1979 to 1994. He received his Th.D. from Wycliffe College, Toronto School of Theology, having studied in the area of historical theology. He regularly teaches at the Toronto Airport Vineyard pastors' and leaders' days, and serves internationally as part of the Airport's renewal team. His first book, *Catch the Fire*, sets what has come to be known as the "Toronto Blessing" in some biblical and historical setting, and complements these studies with present-day testimonies of the impartation of God's grace and love that hundreds of thousands have received through this remarkable outpouring of the Spirit.

Guy is married to Janis; they have two children, Graham and Caitlin. When it's windy enough, Guy is likely to be found out in Lake Ontario, windsurfing.

"Let Your Glory Fall"

David Ruis, Mercy Music, used by permission.

Father of creation, unfold Your sovereign plan
Raise up a chosen generation
That will march through the land
All of creation is longing for Your unveiling of power
Would You release Your anointing
Oh God let this be the hour!

Let Your glory fall in this room
Let it go forth from here to the nations
Let Your fragrance rest in this place
As we gather to seek Your face.

Ruler of the nations, the world has yet to see
The full release of Your promise
The church in victory
Turn to us Lord and touch us
Make us strong in Your might
Overcome our weakness

That we could stand up and fight....
Let Your Kingdom come; *let Your Kingdom come*
Let Your will be done; *let Your will be done*
Let us see on earth; *let us see on earth*
The glory of Your Son....

Guy Chevreau

PRAY WITH FIRE
Interceding in the Spirit

Preface by John Arnott, Senior Pastor of the Toronto
Airport Vineyard

HarperPerennial
HarperCollins*PublishersLtd*

Quotations are taken from the Revised English Bible.

Excerpts from *God's Empowering Presence*, by Gordon Fee are reprinted by permission of Hendrickson Publishers. Copyright © 1994 by Gordon Fee.

Excerpts from *The Life of Saint Theresa*, by E. Allison Peers are reprinted by permission of Sheed & Ward. Copyright © 1991 by E. Allison Peers.

Excerpts from *The Life of Saint Theresa of Avila by Herself*, translated by J.M. Cohen are reprinted by permission of Penguin Books Ltd. Copyright © 1957 by J.M. Cohen.

"Let Your Glory Fall" by David Ruis. Copyright © 1993 Mercy Publishing. Used by permission.

"Save Us Oh God" by Kevin Prosch. Copyright © 1991 Mercy Publishing. Used by permission.

First edition: 1995

Canadian Cataloguing in Publication Data

Chevreau, Guy
  Pray with fire

Includes bibliographical references.
ISBN 0-00-638490-0

1. Toronto Airport Vineyard (Church).   2. Religious awakening – Christianity.   3. Baptism in the Holy Spirit.   I. Title.

BV3777.C3C44 1995   269'.09713'541   C95-931379-6

---

95 96 97 98 99 ❖ HC 10 9 8 7 6 5 4 3 2 1

Printed and bound in the United States

DEDICATION

Pray with Fire is dedicated to all those who serve their brothers and sisters as they intercede in the Spirit. Special thanks go to those of the ministry team of the Toronto Airport Vineyard: bless you for your faithfulness, your kindness, gentleness, and love.

CONTENTS

PREFACE

Prayer is unarguably one of the most important disciplines of the Christian faith. "More things are wrought by prayer than this world dreams of," pleads Alfred Lord Tennyson. The situation though is all too typical. While giving mental and verbal assent as to its importance, Tennyson is not, however, noted for his faithful, disciplined and effective prayer life. Most of us can relate only too well.

In my own case, the struggle has been desperate and intense. There have been seasons of wonderful times "in the closet" with my Heavenly Father, praying to Him in secret and being rewarded by Him openly. During such times, one feels that everything is working out for the good, and one wonders why we could ever be so foolish as to not spend generous hours in communion with God. Then suddenly the cares of this life descend with such fury that the newfound prayer route is derailed once more, and the battle to regain it continues. During the past eighteen months, both Carol and I have been riding this roller coaster and desperately longing for the intimacy with God that goes with a simpler lifestyle and a much less busy schedule.

The renewal at the Airport Vineyard continues nightly. As of June 1995, we estimate that we would have had perhaps 150,000 different people, with a total cumulative attendance of over 400,000. Prayer and intercession has grown to four afternoons a week. My only regret is that I have not had more time in personal prayer.

Dr. Guy Chevreau has been a continual part of the renewal team at the Airport Vineyard ever since it broke out in January 1994. The waters of renewal and revival have been, for us, uncharted as the "Toronto Blessing" begins to make a worldwide impact. Guy's theological and historical perspectives have been a tremendous help to me personally as well as to our entire team and the countless thousands of visitors and leaders. His scholarly and insightful input has time and again been extremely helpful and encouraging to us all.

As the fires of renewal spread, it has been our privilege to see thousands impacted by the Spirit of God. In Toronto, and as we travel extensively to the cities around the world, we see powerful anointing for intercession come upon the people. God is desiring to take all of us to much greater levels of power on the one hand, and much greater depths of intimacy on the other, while at the same time, increasing both our discernment and our revelations that we are receiving.

In his new book, *Pray with Fire*, Guy Chevreau calls us into such a place with God. He calls us to pray with childlike simplicity and sincerity, yet at the same time to be effectual and fervent, as our hearts are stirred by the Holy Spirit. May we never be satisfied with any emotional substitute, or with a "one size fits all" strategy for "revival" or church growth. We are never to lose our perspective of God's sovereign and mysterious ways. He comes suddenly, yet faithfully, to bring His kingdom to a broken and needy world, and as He does so, He generously and graciously includes us.

John Arnott
Senior Pastor
Vineyard Christian Fellowship, Toronto Airport

ACKNOWLEDGEMENTS

A year ago, I resigned the baptist church we were attempting to plant. For many reasons, it was not, nor would be, viable. With my family, we stepped into nothing but God.

It has been quite a year! I spent last summer reading and writing; through a providentially intercepted phone call, HarperCollins UK ended up publishing the work I had intended to self-publish in the hope that my research would serve the pastors and leaders who were coming to the renewal meetings at the Toronto Airport Vineyard. *Catch the Fire* has gone farther than I had ever imagined it might. So have I, having been invited to teach in Switzerland, England, Ireland, Australia, South Africa, Scotland, Finland, Wales, and several cities in Canada and the United States.

I have never known so much of the grace of God, so much of His kindness and faithfulness. I continually shake my head and say out loud, "Thank you, Lord." I have never known so much of the love and generosity of God's people. To the Toronto Airport Vineyard staff and church, and to all my international hosts, I bless you in the name of Jesus.

All this has meant a very different rhythm for our

family. Janis, I bless you for your willingness to embrace all that this call has meant for us. I'm grateful for the increased sense of partnership we have, and we both know that I will never know all that your help has meant. Graham and Caitlin, you are such cherished and precious gifts. I love you so very much.

Thanks also go to Ian Ross, Jeremy Sinnott, Mary Audrey Raycroft and Dr. Chris Page for their comments on the drafts of *Pray with Fire*. You each added significant quality to the work.

Final thanks go to Alan Wiseman, whose faithful intercessions and prophetic encouragement continue to teach me what it means to intercede in the Spirit.

Oakville, Ontario
June 1995

FINDING OURSELVES IN THE MIDST

A Prologue

The whole earth will be full of the knowledge of the Lord's glory as the waters fill the sea. (Habakkuk 2.14)

*   *   *

During our bedtime reading at home, we've been working our way through *Winnie the Pooh*. In "Eeyore has a Birthday," the beloved bear asks Owl to write a note for him, because Pooh is going to give Eeyore a Useful Pot to Keep Things In. Pooh asks for the help because, he says: "My spelling is Wobbly. It's good spelling, but it Wobbles, and the letters get in the wrong places."[1] That spirit of recognized humility is one of the things that makes Pooh so lovable. It is also a very healthy posture to assume when attempting to write a book about prayer. Roughly eighteen hundred years ago, one of the greatest minds of Christendom made humble recognition of

---

[1] A. A. Milne, *Winnie the Pooh* (London, Methuen Children's Books, 1974) p. 73.

1

his need. Origen begins his exposition of the Lord's Prayer by stating the following:

> The discussion of prayer is so great a task that it requires the Father to reveal it, His Firstborn Word to teach it, and the Spirit to enable us to think and speak rightly of so great a subject. That is why I, who am only a human being and in no way attribute an understanding of prayer to myself, think it right to pray for the Spirit before beginning my treatise on prayer, in order that the fullest spiritual account may be given to me and that the prayers written in the Gospels may be made clear.[2]

Recognizing my own "wobbliness," I present this work in this same spirit of humility.

* * *

The "Toronto Blessing" is now known virtually around the Christian world. Meetings that are currently held six nights a week at the Toronto Airport Vineyard began 20 January 1994, and have grown unabated, in size, momentum, and, many would say, in anointing. As of 30 June 1995, somewhere around four hundred thousand people have formed the congregations that average twelve hundred per night, and

[2] *Origen on Prayer—Classics of Western Spirituality*, trans. Rowan Greer (New York, Paulist Press, 1979) p. 86.

are drawn from literally every corner of the globe and virtually every denomination of the Body of Christ. A vast majority of those who come spiritually hungry have experienced a depth of spiritual refreshment, even awakening, such that they conclude that they have touched a precious measure of God's grace, and have seen the power of His love, demonstrated in personal ways.

As God has poured out His Spirit, there are typically some physical manifestations that many have never experienced before—hysterical laughter, weeping, the failing of bodily strength, shaking, and the like.

My wife, Janis, and I live forty kilometres west of the Airport Vineyard, and first heard of the happenings ten days into the meetings. While nothing much took place our first night, we did sense that *something* was going on, and so came the following evening. During the course of that meeting, Janis received the joy, and had my own wife not been so overcome with the holy laughter, I would have attended only a couple of meetings, having pompously dismissed what I was witnessing as Vineyard nonsense.

But having been married to Janis for more than twelve years at the time, I couldn't write things off so quickly. Janis has never demonstrated any significant emotional instability: she is not in desperate need of attention; she is not easily persuaded, nor is she subject to either premillennial angst or hysteria. None of the accusations that have come against those who have been dramatically moved at the meetings fit. Though Janis's behaviour was outside our experiential and expectation set, I reluctantly concluded that, given the context, it seemed as if God was doing some unusual, but truly wonderful things in and through my wife, as well as those around us.

This was a concession I came to reservedly. About our fourth or fifth renewal meeting, one of the Vineyard regional overseers, Ron Allen, was introduced, and invited to testify. He was helped up to the microphone, and with a dumb-drunk look on his face, Ron slowly panned the congregation. His mouth dropped open—and for perhaps a minute, he made several attempts to speak. Then, without warning, he fell over sideways.

I could not suppress my cynicism. I muttered, "God doesn't do that to people."

A short time later, I came across Ezekiel 3:26–27. There the Lord says to His prophet: "I shall make your tongue cleave to the roof of your mouth and you will be unable to speak.... But when I have something to say to you, I shall give you back the power of speech." Later still, while researching previous out-pourings of God's Spirit, I came across this account of the Welsh revivalist Richard Owen, written in 1876. Towards the end of a regularly called prayer meeting, Owen announced a hymn, but that's about as far as he got. "Such an awareness of God's presence overpowered him, that he could give only the first couplet. He tried many times to go through the first verse, and

each failure intensified the sense of awe in the congregation."[3]

While similarities exist in the accounts of Ezekiel's
experience and those of Richard Owen and Ron
Allen, no direct analysis can be undertaken. Too many
details are left untold; there is not enough context for
rigid, scientific examination. It seems that something
of what Ezekiel experienced is somewhat like what
Richard Owen and Ron Allen experienced. But that's
all that can be said conclusively. Religious experience
is, by nature, subjective, and is, therefore, not con-
ducive to scientific analysis.

The book *Catch the Fire: The Toronto Blessing* has
helped many process legitimate questions and concerns this move of God has generated. While a study
of the Scriptures and a review of church history can
never prove the validity of current religious experiences, the Word of God always and unfailingly acts as
a compass, pointing us to true north, to God's revelation in Christ. Documents from the historic church
serve as accounts of fellow travellers who have gone
before us, providing us with records of their discover-
ies and dead ends.

In terms of a biblical and historical study of
renewal and revival, it's only marginally helpful to
read that through the ages, people have found their
bodily strength overcome, that they've shaken,

[3] Eifon Evans, *The Welsh Revival of 1904* (Worcester, Evangelical Press
of Wales, 1989) p. 17.

become speechless, or rolled about in hysterics. That, in and of itself, establishes only that some of the weirdness witnessed at the Airport meetings has historic precedent.

What is of consequence are the thoughtful and prayerful reflections that have come up and out of an encounter with the living God, the ways in which the Scriptures are understood, and the ways in which the gospel of Jesus Christ is experienced.

*   *   *

Concurrent with the celebration of the first anniversary of the renewal meetings at the Toronto Airport Vineyard, the *Christian Week* succinctly described the year's events as follows: "A persistent demonstration of supernatural power—signs and wonders including 'holy laughter' and 'slain in the Spirit' experiences—brought spiritual refreshing to thousands of Christians. In the process, a nondescript Toronto area church was transformed into a destination point for pilgrims from all over the world."[4] Without attempting a full list, there are thousands and thousands of folks who have come to one or more of the Airport meetings, and, typically when prayed for, found themselves, as John Wesley described, "being struck down." Thousands have experienced something similar to what Jonathan Edwards spoke of as "omnipotent joy," what Charles Haddon Spurgeon's delightfully

[4] *Christian Week*, 3 January 1995.

described as "extraordinary epilepsy," and what Methodist circuit preacher Peter Cartwright called "the jerks."[5] And while the physical manifestations are what arrest most first-timers' attention, a deeper, more consequential dynamic is at work in "the Toronto Blessing." Considered to be a most remarkable out-pouring of God's Spirit on the Church worldwide, there are unnumbered testimonies of believers from all walks of life who have experienced deep spiritual refreshing, even awakening, and *more*: there has come a gracious impartation of power, anointing, and authority in ministry for God's church.

Encounter with the Living God should have the focus of our attention, and not any particular manifestation or experience. We relate to the Giver, and receive His gifts. But in recognizing how dynamic the manifestations are, our focus frequently gets blurred. During morning teaching times at the Toronto Airport Vineyard, one issue is raised at almost every pastors' and leaders' question session: some people are concerned that they manifest so much and so freely that they feel they can't control themselves; consequently, they feel very self-conscious. Some, at the other end of the spectrum, are concerned because they're not manifesting anything physically, and they wonder, "What's wrong with me?"

John Arnott has addressed some of these concerns

---

[5] See *Catch the Fire*, chapters 4 and 6, for some historical precedents to the manifestations documented in previous revivals.

in a helpful teaching titled "Receiving the Spirit's Power." It is also a chapter in his forthcoming book, *The Father's Blessing*.

One can nuance things further, especially after having prayed for hundreds of men and women. After blessing them in the name of Jesus, one of the things I've learned to look at is the square inch of a person's forehead centred right above the eyes. It usually tells quite a tale. Once Vineyard leaders Randy Clark and Ron Allen had pointed this piece out to me, it was something with which I was only too familiar.

If that square inch looks relaxed, it typically signals a trusting, restful spirit that is waiting on the Lord. It often reflects an attitude of quiet worship, of abandon to whatever the Spirit should impart. If, instead, that square inch is scrunched, the brows knitted, and the rest of the forehead rippled, it often evidences such things as striving, or worry, or fear, or control. Again, I knew this only too well. In the early months of the meetings, there was in me an inclination to scrunch up. By the grace of God, it is one inclination that has diminished considerably.

When I stand before these men and women as one on the ministry team, it's with some understanding and considerable empathy for their internal state that I'll often touch them on the shoulder and suggest that they're working too hard; that they've come forward to receive, and there's nothing for them to do—they're already here. Now it's for God to bless.

Grace is a rascal for some folks to take hold of; some close their eyes again, and scrunch up their foreheads. I touch them on the shoulder a second time and try to help by saying, "This is Christmas. What do you do on Christmas morning?" They often look puzzled, so I keep helping. "You run into the living room, look under the tree, and find the present with your name on it. Are you worried that there isn't something under the tree for you?"

I understand some of the anguish of those who aren't sure, those who have great difficulty believing that there's a carefully chosen gift from their loving Father, who knows exactly how to bless them. For many, their experience has been an experienced "absence" of God, not presence—or His presents. The classic "dark night of the soul" has seemingly lasted for months, if not years. But this outpouring of God's Spirit marks a new season for many of those receiving prayer: it is as the monk Thomas Merton wrote:

> The option of absolute despair is turned into perfect hope by pure and humble supplications. [We] face the worst, and discover in it the hope of the best. From the darkness comes light. From death, life. From the abyss there comes, unaccountably, the mysterious gift of the Spirit sent by God to make all things new, to transform the created and redeemed world, and to re-establish all things in Christ.[6]

[6] Thomas Merton, *Contemplative Prayer* (New York, Image Books, 1969) p. 25.

Sometimes you can see this transformation take place on a person's face: understanding that this is all about *grace*, they quieten their spirits, their foreheads unscrunch, and like Mary's posture before the angel Gabriel, they are able to pray, "Be it to me according to Your word." Or, less eloquently but with a similarly surrendered spirit, "Whatever, Lord." Sometimes they start weeping as the Spirit of God begins releasing very deep pain, lifting some longstanding fears. Sometimes they start laughing as they experience a powerful liberation in the love of the Lord.

Sadly, it seems as if some people can't, or won't, let go of their control. As we return to prayer, some folks scrunch up their foreheads again, and often their spirits get noisy. They start up once more, often frantically praying the name of Jesus or bubbling over in tongues. Speaking as one on the ministry team, I know these are hard cases to pray into. We try to suggest that folks can't kiss and talk at the same time— and so ask which they'd rather do!

* * *

If we scratch around here a little longer, we can trace yet another dynamic at work. It's one of the subtle temptations that bring distortion to this move of the Spirit— name it a "manifestation/anointing/gifts covetousness." "Gee, I'd really like the ... laughter...."

With their foreheads all scrunched up, some have come forward for prayer, but have zeroed in on one particular manifestation or gift. That, and really only that, is what they want. The thing is, if we focus on any one of the ways in which the Spirit manifests the grace of God, and get locked in on whatever, things will derail sooner or later, because the focus has been put on the gift, rather than the Giver of "every good and perfect gift."[7]

In the early months, my wife frequently fell about in hysterics. While this now only occurs on occasion, the laughter was received as a precious gift—as never before, she discovered that the "joy of the Lord is her strength." My good friend Alan has shaken so violently, and for such extended periods of time, that he's broken several folding chairs, popping the rivets right out of them. Often when he and I talk and pray on the phone, he starts shaking so hard that he drops the phone. I've prayed for lots of men and women who have wept and wept and wept. I know a number—a very small percentage—who have roared, and one woman who crowed. What I do most is stand. It's been nicknamed the "oak of righteousness" anointing. Over the past sixteen months I have manifested very little in comparison. Is that okay? Should I be satisfied?

If we get jealous of the ways in which the Spirit's presence and power are manifested in someone else, we may well miss, or even undo, what the Lord is intending to accomplish, not only in our own personal lives but also in His church. This is one of the keys to understanding some of what's happening at

[7] James 1:17.

the Toronto Airport Vineyard, and this gracious and beautiful outpouring of God's Spirit—we're discovering more of what it means to be the Body of Christ, especially as we come a little closer to figuring out who has been given what.

The ministry gifts of Pastor John Arnott and those of the Airport Vineyard staff were joined with those of Randy Clark when he was invited up from St. Louis; since Randy brought with him some of his ministry team, they were further complemented. Vineyard leaders Wes Campbell and Ron Allen brought their gifts to bear as they joined with two men who have prophetic ministries, Larry Randolph and Marc Dupont; and as local pastors from other Vineyards joined with other pastors and leaders from virtually every denominational stripe and colour, there has come a remarkable opportunity to "discern the Body," to pray for one another and receive from one another some of what the Lord purposes to release to and through each of us.

*   *   *

The Apostle Paul describes what the Church is supposed to be like, in Ephesians 4. The chapters that precede it spell out God's larger purpose: in chapter 1, verses 8 and 9, for instance, Paul speaks of "God's secret purpose." In verse 10, he declares that purpose: "that the universe, everything in heaven and on earth, might be brought into a unity in Christ." That so many believers should gather together without denominational strife or intrigue is one of the dynamics at the Airport Vineyard that has captured the attention of the secular world. This unity is what many outside the Church think things ought to look like if we're really taking the message of Jesus seriously. Within the Church, many are learning in new ways that their "Lone Ranger" Christianity—that individualistic, "me and Jesus" pride that keeps them distant and disconnected from their brothers and sisters—has not served them, the Body, or the mission to which we are called.

With that as preface, Ephesians 4 now has some context. The citation begins with verse 3, and runs through verse 13.

Each of us has been given a special gift, a particular share in the bounty of Christ. When He [the Lord] ascended into heaven, He gave gifts to us all.... It is He who has given some to be apostles, some prophets, some to be evangelists, some pastors and teachers, to equip God's people for work in His service, until we all attain to the unity inherent in our faith and in our knowledge of the Son of God—to mature manhood, measured by nothing less than the full stature of Christ.

I quite think I'd like the holy laughter. I even think I'd like to shake some or jerk a bit, and *know* the power of the Lord on me. The roaring I'm not sure about;

the screaming I think I'd just as soon leave well enough alone.

Wrong.

We so easily choose what we'd most like, and quickly try to make sense of what this outpouring of God's Spirit means for us personally. "What is God up to in my life?" Recognizing that the working of grace in our lives deserves reflection, we also need to discern what the Spirit seems to be calling forth in and through us as He calls us into greater unity as the Body of Christ. It would serve us all well if we could spend less energy trying to figure out which of the manifestations we'd most "like," and even spend a little less time trying to figure out what God is doing in us as He pours out His Spirit, and instead work towards understanding how it is that the Lord is building and equipping His Body, the Church. Most of us are far too individualistic in our understanding of spiritual gifts, the manifestations of His presence and power, and the work of the Spirit renewing and reviving the Church.

My wife got the laughter, and a further release and gifting of compassion, faith, hope, and authority. That's more than evidenced as she joins with others on the ministry team and prays for folks. My friend Alan continues to shake violently, and is now further released in the prophetic ministry the Lord is calling forth within him. I receive him as a precious gift, as do many others, for he encourages, and stimulates, and strengthens me with his intercessions, and the visions and insights he brings to bear on the conduct of my ministry, and the others for whom he is interceding.

Again, in terms of manifestations, what I do most is stand; but when I received prayer while beginning to write *Catch the Fire*, my left index finger twitched for two days. In faith, I received even that little bit as an anointing for prophetic typing!

Janis laughs, and Alan jerks; neither of them gets to sift through church history and write the way I get to. I hope and pray that the ways in which the Spirit is manifesting grace in my life serves as a blessing to the Body, His Church.

* * *

As I have continued to research the historic outpourings of God's Spirit, I came across the following, a declaration that could have been penned at any number of the Airport Vineyard meetings. It is written by a leader of Welsh Pentecostalism, Daniel Williams, and dates from around 1914. Williams's reflections not only serve as a descriptive record of what was being experienced, but also evidence gracious pastoral wisdom and discernment.

> The manifestation of the power was beyond human management. Men and women were mowed down by the axe of God like a forest. The glory was resting for over two years in some localities. Ministers could not minister, like Moses, when the cloud of glory came down on

the Tabernacle. The weeping for mercy, the holy laughter, ecstasy of joy, the fire descending, burning its way to the hearts of men and women with sanctity and glory, were manifestations still cherished and longed for in greater power. Many were heard speaking in tongues and prophesying. Many witnessed God's healing power in their bodies. Confusion and extravagance, undoubtedly, were present. But the Lord had His hand on His people, and they were preserved and were taught of God to persevere and pray.

Gradually the gifts were again manifested. The voice of God was heard ... and, the voice, with no uncertain sound to its hearers, was opening new doors, and the Pentecostal flame ran through the country, and is still spreading.[8]

This book, *Pray with Fire,* is subtitled *Interceding in the Spirit.* It is not so much about praying for revival, as it is praying *in the midst* of revival. It is hoped that it will serve as a resource to those who find themselves used of God to be the conduits, and the vehicles, of His blessing.

In this we can consider our prayers of intercession to be somewhere on a continuum. On one end are the very simple requests that have characterized much of what is prayed at the Toronto Airport Vineyard: "Fill with Your Spirit"; "More, Lord."

[8] Evans, p. 194.

These are the shortest of prayers, that one be filled with the Holy Spirit, as the Apostle admonishes in Ephesians 5:18, "be filled with the Holy Spirit"; that there be more, "immeasurably more than we can ask or conceive, by the power of the Spirit at work in our midst," as in the Apostle's prayer in Ephesians 3:20–21. These short prayers with functional simplicity have noteable historical precedent. Evans Roberts, the recognized leader of the Welsh revival that began in 1904, laid down these guidelines for meetings he was called on to conduct:

> Establish revival meetings there, call all the denominations together. Explain the "four conditions"; and at the end of the meeting let all who have confessed Christ remain behind, and initiate the round of ejaculatory prayer. Take care that each one prays:
>
> 1. Send the Spirit now, for Jesus Christ's sake.
> 2. Send the Spirit powerfully now, for Jesus Christ's sake.
> 3. Send the Spirit more powerfully now, for Jesus Christ's sake.
> 4. Send the Spirit still more powerfully now, for Jesus Christ's sake.[9]

With such simple prayers and brevity, God's sovereign grace and kindness have once again been poured out,

[9] Evans, p. 99.

such that thousands have experienced a most remarkable blessing and a radical transformation of life.

On the other end of the continuum, a prophetic revelation reads "the secrets of the heart."[10] Articulated with precision, there is in these intercessions a timely particularity that speaks Heart to heart into a person's history, both the now and tomorrow of a person's life. Having been the subject of several sessions of this kind of prayer ministry, I have no doubt that this prophetic, revelatory ministry, when exercised by humble, anointed men and women, is blessed by God to "build up, stimulate and encourage."[11]

Once recognized, however, it is frustrating to many that there is in all of this no methodology. No training manual or binder is provided at the Airport Vineyard leaders' days. There are no "Ten Ways" or "Twelve Keys" that can be categorized and systematized. What follows is a brief look at the prayer ministry of the Toronto Airport Vineyard as it has developed since the first of the meetings in early 1994. In subsequent chapters, some biblical instruction is brought to bear, as well as some historic reflections on prayer that may serve as guiding metaphors and principles, as we offer ourselves to be used of the Spirit to intercede for our brothers and sisters, that "the whole earth be filled with the glory of the Lord."[12]

[10] 1 Corinthians 14:25.
[11] 1 Corinthians 14:3.
[12] Habakkuk 2:14.

CHAPTER TWO

WALKING IN GOD'S LOVE AND GIVING IT AWAY

Toronto Airport Vineyard Update

Give, and gifts will be given to you. Good measure, pressed and shaken down and running over, will be poured into your lap; for whatever measure you deal out to others will be dealt to you in turn. (Luke 6:38)

*   *   *

The meetings at the Toronto Airport Vineyard have generated a considerable amount of media attention, both Christian and secular. The various headlines and story profiles create a mosaic, as friends, foes, and indifferents make their assessments of a ministry that is characterized by four fundamental movements: corporate worship that is expectant, hopeful, and praise filled; testimonies from several individuals who believe they've experienced something more of the Grace of God; simple gospel exhortation and invitation; and intercessory prayer that is Spirit attentive and directive, as brothers and sisters in the Lord pray for one another.

With a clever play on words, the Canadian magazine *Faith Today* titled their cover story "After the

Laughter." The article begins: "'To walk in God's love, and give it away.' When the leadership of the Airport Vineyard Christian Fellowship developed this mission statement, they had no idea how much controversy receiving God's love would create."[1]

Toronto Life, a glitzy monthly filled with high-life advertising, had this in its December 1994 "Best and worst: a year in the life of the city":

> Most notable tourist attraction! A rumour spread throughout the Christian world that the Lord had taken up residence at Toronto Airport Vineyard. True believers are flocking from all over the world.

In the February issue, *Toronto Life* ran a follow-up article: "God is Alive and Well and Saving Souls on Dixon Road." The journalist, who spent considerable time at several meetings, interviewing staff and members of the renewal team, brought forth a cocky, cynical, even cheeky report; with surprising candour, he confessed he was nonetheless unsettled by his time at the Airport: "The plain truth is that I can't explain what I saw that night...."

* * *

Dr. Andrew MacRae, principal of Acadia Divinity College, reviewed *Catch the Fire* in the monthly magazine *The Atlantic Baptist*. Acadia was the college from

[1] *Faith Today*, March 1995, p. 19.

which I received my Master of Divinity degree; I studied under Andrew my last year there.

In his review Andrew writes:

Catch the Fire tells the boisterous story of a local gathering of Christian enthusiasts who have shared some wild and very strange experiences, which has drawn vast numbers of people from around the world to see the phenomena, to catch the fire, to enter into the experience, to find a new way of uninhibited, unusual and very long praise and worship.... Like every preceding generation, we tend to be drawn to the sensational, whether it be a sensational advertisement, a sensational film, a sensational miracle, or a sensational sign. And the present clamour by charismatic Christians from around the world to go to Toronto is much more typical of our age than it is of our Lord.[2]

With less anticharismatic prejudice evidenced, John Stackhouse named several concerns, and concluded his critique with these words:

It remains evident that many, many people around the world are today rejoicing in the Lord Jesus Christ more than they were before because

---

[2] *The Atlantic Baptist*, Andrew MacRae, "The Toronto Blessing: An Experience of Renewal and Revival." February, 1995. pp. 12-13

of their encounter with God's Spirit at the Airport Vineyard. As we go to church this week, to our small-group fellowships, to our family prayers, to our private devotions, we may not follow their path. Indeed we may criticize it.

But if we do, we had better consider whether we have a genuine alternative that offers people an authentic and transforming encounter with God. We may legitimately prefer something different, but we dare not be content with less.[3]

The "Toronto Blessing" was the cover story of February's *Charisma* magazine; its title asked: "What is God doing in Toronto?" When the issue was first released and the question was read from the front of the church, one of the women on the ministry team, leaned over to me and quipped with a grin, "He's doing whatever He wants!"

* * *

As the news clips demonstrate, reaction to the meetings has generated a varied response. When the Airport Vineyard moved from the industrial unit on the west side of Pearson International Airport to the bankrupt Asian Trade Centre on Attwell Drive to the east, the *Toronto Star*, rarely kind to the Church, was

[3] John Stackhouse, "Encounters at Vineyard," *Christian Week*, 20 September 1994. John is the associate professor of Modern Christianity, Department of Religion, University of Manitoba.

impressed enough with the integrity they perceived to title a sidebar headline "They're not empire building, not at this point at least."[4]

The move was precipitated only by the fact that since the summer of 1994, the Dixon Road facility simply could not accommodate the more than eight hundred people who arrived night after night through the autumn of 1994. Since the prophetic conference that was held in November and the move to Attwell, attendance has averaged at least twelve hundred a night; through anniversary week, evening attendances peaked at four thousand.

Denominational leaders from around the world have been sufficiently impressed with the humility and anointing of the leadership of the Airport renewal team to invite them to minister at conferences in England, Scotland, Wales, Ireland, Norway, Holland, Sweden, Finland, Switzerland, Germany, France, Thailand, Japan, Mexico, South Africa, Australia, New Zealand, Egypt, Israel, and throughout North America. The simple dynamics of expectant worship, revival preaching, and Spirit-attentive prayer are easily transferrable, and as God's blessing is sought, renewal, refreshing, awakening, and release break out.

* * *

The senior pastor of the Airport Vineyard, John Arnott, and his wife, Carol, are away one-third to

4 *Toronto Star*, 3 December 1994, p. A24.

one-half the time, responding to invitations to come and serve as anointed fire lighters in centres all around the world. In a way, their absence from the Airport meetings doesn't matter. The staff and leadership of the church are gifted and mature—thousands have come and gone while the Arnotts have been away, and they have left the Airport greatly blessed. On a few occasions, not a single Airport staff person has been at the meetings. "Friends of renewal," either local or a team from away, take the lead, and again God continues to pour out His blessing, irrespective of the presence or absence of the senior pastor and staff. It would be a completely different story if the ministry team were absent. John and Carol could be present, but they would not be able to give the kind of time and prayerful attention to the hundreds and hundreds who come to receive prayer. Night after night, it's the men and women wearing the ministry team sticker badges who serve so faithfully, as they pray for those who come to receive the blessing of their Lord.

As has been recognized, the "family" functions well even when "Mom and Dad" Arnott are away on business. However, a wonderful dynamic is at work when they're back home. It's not so much that there is a greater anointing on the ministry at times when the Arnotts are present as there is a greater ease and sense of security, a recognition of the loving watch-care and oversight that are the Arnotts' to bring to bear.

The ministry teams are what differentiate this outpouring from many other renewal ministries; they certainly distinguish the "Toronto Blessing" from the meetings of another contemporary renewal leader, Rodney Howard Browne. It is not the "anointed man of God" doing the ministry, but rather, as John Arnott describes it, a "nameless, faceless" move of the Spirit, where brothers and sisters in Christ pray for one another.

Including staff, there were between forty and fifty original members of the ministry team at the Toronto Airport Vineyard when things began 20 January 1994. As the crowds grew those first weeks, the pastoral responsibilities were quickly recognized. People were coming to receive prayer, and the goal was to create as safe and as healthy an environment as possible. It was freely acknowledged that with all the pastors and leaders who were gathering, there were some at the meetings who could pray circles around the ministry team. The thing was that most of the Airport's "guests" were strangers, and as such the leadership at the Airport did not yet know their hearts.

For that reason, the ministry team was issued pink sticker tags, a practice that continues today. Only they are released to pray for those who come forward, because those on ministry team *are* known by Airport staff, and they have every confidence in the spirit-attentive quality of ministry that will be given. To signal the commitment to integrity and accountability, the names of the ministry team personnel were subsequently added; the congregation is told that if they feel they've been pushed, or if they feel that the ministry they've received is inappropriate, they should open their eyes, read the name on the tag, and come speak with the ministry team captain.

This very rarely happens because of the careful training the ministry team receives. The original team members had participated in several spiritual gifts and prophetic conferences, worked through inner healing materials, as well as deliverance and spiritual warfare training courses. Robert McGee's book, *Search for Significance,* has served as the textbook for the ministry team. It addresses issues of self-worth, approval, and performance, and in the workbook section it gives biblical grounding for significance in the love, acceptance, and unconditional forgiveness of Jesus.[5]

* * *

As the meetings continued month after month, more and more people were required on the ministry team. More than two hundred now serve, with roughly thirty percent of them coming from other local churches. A further ten percent are from other area Vineyards.

Visiting teams, from the greater Toronto area have come in and taken the meetings; teams from Dallas, Manhattan, Fort Wayne, Seattle, Three Cities, and

[5] Robert McGee, *Search for Significance* (Houston, Rapha Publishing, 1990).

Sacramento have visited, sometimes for a week at a time, giving the leadership and ministry team at the Airport Vineyard a well-deserved rest!

As the training and stickering of the ministry team addressed some of the spiritual responsibilities generated by the numbers of people coming forward for prayer, similar concerns for their physical safety were raised. Now every ministry team member is supposed to work with a "catcher," someone who will stand behind the person receiving prayer and ease him to the floor should he find it too difficult to stand any longer. Visiting pastors are especially encouraged to volunteer to catch, because it's an excellent opportunity to overhear the praying and apprentice in this school of ministry.

The point is made repeatedly: catchers are called for not because there is the expectation that people will fall down when prayed for, but rather to protect those who are already on the floor, since they're usually the ones who get hurt if somebody falls without a catcher. If a person goes uncaught, it's the already resting eye that suffers the newly felled elbow!

* * *

Some of the questions that have arisen out of the "Toronto Blessing" are "What's normative?" "What ought we to be expecting in terms of worship, preaching, and ministry, and the ways in which we receive and understand the Lord to be powerfully present in our midst?" "Is all of this a blip on the scales, and sooner or later, we'll return to normal?" "If so, what's normal?" The questions are not new ones. The revival scholar Iain Murray reflects on the "quieter" decades following the Great Awakening:

> What happens in revivals is not to be seen as something miraculously different from the regular experience of the church. The difference lies in degree, not in kind. In an "outpouring of the Spirit" spiritual influence is more widespread, convictions are deeper, and feelings more intense, but all this is only a heightening of normal Christianity. True revivals are "extraordinary", yet what is experienced at such times is not different in essence from the spiritual experience that belongs to Christians at other times. It is the larger "earnest" of the same spirit who abides with all those who believe.... What characterizes a revival is not the employment of unusual or special means but rather the extraordinary degree of blessing attending the normal means of grace.[6]

One of the Baptist preachers in the Second Great Awakening, Robert Turnbull, brought these reflections to bear: "The Lord seems to have stepped out of the usual path of ordinances, to effect this work more immediately

---

[6] Iain Murray, *Revival and Revivalism: The Making and Marring of American Evangelicalism* (Edinburgh, Banner of Truth Trust, 1994) pp. 23 and 129.

in the displays of His Almighty power, and outpouring of His Spirit; probably to show that the work is His own."[7] This is particularly the case when we consider "normal" prayer, and what it means to "intercede in the Spirit." Regardless of its fervency, frequency, and community, prayer is no guarantor of results. Back in 1866, the revival preacher Gardiner Spring affirmed: "Revivals are always spurious when they are *got up* by man's device, and not *brought down* by the Spirit of God."[8]

There is clear understanding and confession that what has been experienced in the "Toronto Blessing" is grace, a gift given at the Lord's sovereign initiative, and that God's grace and this outpouring of His Spirit have increased the intensity and fervency of corporate intercession.

Pastor Ian Ross came on staff at the Airport Vineyard in September 1993, and one of his responsibilities was to promote and oversee the church's ministry of intercession. Ian found that this kind of prayer only took place in the home kinship groups. Sunday by Sunday, he would plead with the congregation to come to intercessory prayer meetings. Few would respond.

At one meeting that autumn, only Shirley Smith was able to join Ian for prayer. While he was grumbling and complaining to God, Shirley sensed that the

[7] C.R. Keller, *Second Great Awakening in Connecticut* (New Haven, Yale University Press, 1942) p. 195.
[8] Murray, p. 201.

Lord was saying that He wanted to "call in" the intercessors, to "birth" intercession in their midst.
Together they felt that they were to pray over the
empty seats of the sanctuary, to prepare the way.
Unbeknown to them, the following Sunday John
Arnott preached on intercession. When he invited
those who would give themselves to this ministry,
dozens responded.

Since 20 January 1994, the intercessory meetings
have continued to grow. As of March 1995, between a
hundred and four hundred people gather for about two
hours on four afternoons a week. The time is devoted
to waiting on God. After inviting the Spirit to come
and direct their intercessions, the leaders—Ian and
Shirley, Verda and Jean—encourage words of knowledge, prophetic pictures, dance, and spiritual songs.

There have been some wonderful surprises.
Recently, Dutch visitors were reconciled with their
German brothers in the Lord, as they both repented
of longstanding animosity, even hatred of each
other's nations.

On another occasion, a gentleman entered the
room by accident. He was not a believer, but was
intrigued with the presence he was sensing. He asked
what the meeting was about. Some folks led him to
the Lord and prayed that he would be filled with the
Holy Spirit. As he rested in the Lord's love, the intercessions carried on.

Ian says of the meetings: "There is a sense that we
are just at the beginning, still learning how to pray

faithfully through what is on God's heart. There is still need for more prayer, for God to draw more of those whom He has called to intercession. May He burden more to come and join together in prayer, asking Him to bring His Kingdom to a lost world."

CHAPTER THREE

REVELATORY MINISTRY

In the Gospel of John, the Acts of the Apostles,
and the Letters of the Apostle Paul

Flesh gives birth only to flesh;
it is Spirit that gives birth to spirit. (John 3:6)

*   *   *

Since the early days of the renewal meetings, John
Wimber, the Association of Vineyard Churches'
International director, has given the leadership at the
Airport Vineyard ongoing pastoral oversight and counsel. While there are times when the manifestations
require some apologetic and theological reflection, John
has repeatedly called for the "main, plain things of
Scripture" to have and hold the focus of concern. To
that end, *Catch the Fire* sought to lay a foundation for
the "Toronto Blessing" that was grounded on the manifest presence of God and the sovereign initiative that
God takes in revealing Himself, such that His people
see, hear, and feel His presence with us. These revelations are the very core of biblical and historical faith, for
without these encounters, we would have only what was
termed in the Middle Ages *Deus Absconditus*, the God
who is far off and uninvolved in the living of our lives.

The Scriptures, however, are an extended chroni-
cling of those times and seasons when God "descends,"
"appears," and "makes His face shine upon us." In
Jesus, God "takes flesh and dwells among us," and by
an impartation of His Spirit, He is "with us always."
The Lord's ongoing self-disclosure is so central to
Christian faith that we can speak of a "theology of
presence," such that we find *ourselves* called by name
and drawn into ever-deepening friendship with God.
The purpose of this chapter is to build on this work,
for we consider prayer as the means by which we
receive and respond to the Lord's gracious initiatives.

* * *

Throughout the Old Testament, a number of
extended prayers of intercession are recorded, in
which God's people cry out for mercy and blessing,
for release from shame, and forgiveness of sin.
Abraham, Moses, Solomon, Nehemiah, David, and
Daniel are among those who interceded for the corporate well-being of their nation, calling forth restoration and revival.[1]

By God's grace, we find ourselves not so much
praying *for* as living *in the midst* of what has historically been called a season of awakening. As such, a different set of questions are raised with respect to our
understanding and practice of prayer.

[1] See Genesis 18:19–33; Exodus 32:30–34, 33:12–23; 2 Chronicles
6:12–7.2; Nehemiah 1:4–11; Psalms 80 and 85; Daniel 9:3–27.

As were the majority of evangelicals, I was brought up with an understanding of prayer that was based essentially on the rhythm of withdrawal and work recorded in Mark 1:35: "Very early the next morning [Jesus] got up and went out. He went away to a remote spot and remained there in prayer." Texts like this form the basis for the classic quiet time before one rushes out into the involvements of a busy life— and as is sometimes conveyed, it carries overtones of the old deodorant commercial, "One shot, and you're good for the whole day."

That doesn't exactly qualify as a life of prayer. Through the writings of Thomas Merton and Henri Nouwen, to name only two, the contemplative disciplines of silence, solitude, and Scripture meditation have been a welcome addition to a quick read of the day's Bible chapter, and then on to a few minutes of adoration, confession, thanksgiving, and supplication—framed on the mnemonic aid ACTS.

Since 20 January 1994 and the outpouring of God's Spirit at the first of the Toronto Airport Vineyard meetings, many have found themselves in a very different situation, asking, "What does it mean to be praying in the midst of awakening and revival?" As the men and women of the ministry team gather to serve their brothers and sisters who come forward for prayer, night after night, what does it mean for them to "intercede in the Spirit"? Some nights, there are more than a thousand people wanting prayer, and only a handful on the ministry team. Faced with what sometimes seems overwhelming need, the classic Vineyard prayer serves time and again: "Oh God! Oh God!" There is complete and absolute dependence on the resources that the Lord alone gives—ministry team members are so overwhelmed with the graciousness of God that they are quick to confess it is certainly not their experience or technical ability that touches the hearts and transforms the lives of those who come for prayer.

This awareness, and the experience of the presence and power of God, is at the heart of all that is prayed for at the Toronto Airport Vineyard. If we were to bring forward a single word to describe all that is entailed, it would simply be *more*. More of the Word of God with power. In Ephesians 3:16, the Apostle prays "that out of the treasures of [the Father's] glory He may grant you inward strength and power through His Spirit...." The Greek is awkward to translate, it literally means: "power to become mighty through the Spirit of Him (Jesus) in the inward man." If things were amplified a little, the text would read "In Jesus, it is God's pleasure and purpose to pour into our heart of hearts the power to become mighty through His Spirit." This is not spiritual self-actualization; this is not might in and for ourselves. God pours out His Spirit so that we become mighty for Kingdom ministry—for service: so we can be praying for the sick and the oppressed; so we can preach the good news with boldness, faith, and authority; so we can care for the poor and work for justice and righteousness. If we were to employ a shorthand for that, we could call it *prophetic ministry.*

This would need to be differentiated from doom and gloom, timetable predictions and prognostications. There is very little of that in the prophetic arena that the New Testament evidences. In the early Church, prophetic ministry was essentially *release*, such that more of God and more of His purposes are revealed. It is the might and the power of the Spirit God, at work in and through believers, such that when they move "prophetically," people receive from them more than what they on their own can possibly give. It's an indispensable piece when it comes to ministry, mission, and especially evangelism, Prophetic ministry is a function of the revelatory, the revealing of God, and His redemptive, re-creative, restorative purposes for us as His people, and for us as Christ's Body.

* * *

I continue to return to James Dunn's book, *Jesus and the Spirit*, for I find it to be one of my ten "desert island library" choices. In his study of the Apostle Paul and prophecy, he works with texts like 1 Corinthians 14:1: "Make love your aim; then be eager for the gifts of the Spirit, above all for prophecy." He asks, "Why is prophecy so important for Paul?" The one sentence answer is, "Because it builds up the assembly." Having asked why, I expected him to move on to how—"How does prophecy build up the assembly?" But surprisingly, Dunn really doesn't ask the question; he certainly doesn't work very hard at answering it.

I worked through Wayne Grudem's book, *The Gift of Prophecy in the New Testament and Today*, thinking that maybe he would answer the question. Grudem's work is a helpful study of the prophetic in the early church. The trouble is, the book is mistitled, because after Grudem spends some time on Old Testament prophecy, he dives into Paul's instructions on the prophetic in 1 Corinthians. Chapter 4 is titled "New Testament Prophets in the Rest of the New Testament." I read that chapter, and flipped through the rest of the book and the Scripture indices, only to find that Grudem doesn't give any consideration to the prophetic ministry of Jesus! In fact, most commentators simply do not have the revelatory ministry of Jesus on their interpretive horizons.

Especially in the midst of this outpouring of God's Spirit, and the release of the prophetic that accompanies it, an understanding of the prophetic ministry of Jesus is an essential piece to understanding how it is that the prophetic builds up the church. If "out of the treasures of His glory," God takes pleasure in giving us the "power to become mighty through the Spirit of Jesus in our innermost beings,"[2] then it seems like a serious oversight to neglect the prophetic ministry of Jesus.

Believing that it makes sense to study how the Master moved in the revelatory as we try apprenticing in this school, the following is a study of the revelatory ministry of Jesus in the Fourth Gospel.

[2] Ephesians 3:16.

The Apostle John begins his prologue with the words "In the beginning was the Word." In English "word" is a fairly neutral, static, nondescript lump. The Greek for "word" is *logos*, but that doesn't help most of us. We get all philosophic and heady. The Hebrew root is *davar*, which is best understood as "divine self-expression," an "event." God speaks and something happens. Things are no longer as they were; creation comes out of chaos and confusion. The romance languages serve us well by way of translation—in Spanish, the opening verse reads *En el principio era el Verbo....* "In the beginning was the verb." Jesus is Himself the Word of God with power.

In John 1:9, we read that "the true light which gives light to everyone was even then coming into the world." This giving of light implies enlightenment—to illuminate inwardly. But it is not so much general revelation, as in Romans 1:20, or a repeat of John 1:4, but the cartoon light bulb—aha! That's why Jesus has come—so we get it. Time and again, as we've prayed for men and women these past eighteen months, this "true light" shines forth, night after night. The light bulb goes on, and folks know, as never before, that the Lord is for them and not against; that God is their Father, and Jesus their Saviour, that there is communion with the Holy Spirit. Just before I left an evening meeting in Sydney, Australia, a man I had prayed for earlier expressed his gratitude with these simple words: "Thank you for helping me to experience the love of Jesus as never before." Aha.

In John 1:16, it is declared that "from His full store, we have received grace upon grace." The New International Version translates "grace upon grace" as "one blessing after another." Again, while in Australia, our hosts took us to Nousa Beach north of Brisbane—the head of a a magnificent beach that extends sixty-five miles. As I spent the day there, the Pacific Ocean stretching out for six thousand miles, this text kept sounding and resounding in my ears: "From His full store, we have received grace upon grace." From His full store—the Pacific Ocean—we have received wave after wave after wave of grace. Grace piled on grace upon grace. The sweet wind of God's Spirit is blowing; big swell is rolling in. The power of God's love is building, and as it comes, it breaks on the shores of our lives. This is no rogue wave, a one-time deal; no—the wind of God's Spirit generates break after break, wave after wave after wave, grace upon grace upon grace.

The conclusion to the introduction of the gospel reads "No one has ever seen God; God's only Son, He who is nearest to the Father's heart, He has made him known."[3] The Greek word translated as "known" is rendered literally in English as "exegete," meaning to lead, guide, to show, to explain. This is a generic, broad-stroke declaration of the Lord's ministry, the "frame" to John's gospel. From here on out, John will be painting the canvas inside this frame. What John

[3] John 1:18.

wants to make clear at the very beginning is that the purpose of Jesus's coming is to reveal the Father. To make Him known. We see Jesus, and we see the "human face of God." John is telling us here that Jesus reveals more of God than has ever been revealed; that by its very nature, the ministry of Jesus is *prophetic*: one long, ongoing revelation.

* * *

Now down to specifics. At Jesus's baptism at the river Jordan, John the Baptist testifies: "I saw the Spirit come down from heaven like a dove and come to rest on Him."[4] So translated, one could mistakenly imagine that there is now a pretty white bird perched on Jesus's shoulder, a sort of sanctified "Captain Hook and Polly" deal. The translation would be better, stronger if it spoke of the Spirit *remaining* on Jesus, as the New International and Revised Standard translations do, because what Jesus does through the course of His ministry, He does under the influence of the Spirit who is ever with Him. To use the Apostle Paul's words from Ephesians 3:16, it is the Spirit that gives Jesus "the power to be mighty."

There's more. In verse 3, John the Baptist says: "The One on whom you see the Spirit come down and remain is the One who is to baptize in Holy Spirit." From the very beginning of the Lord's ministry, a superabundance of the Spirit is anticipated.

[4] John 1:32.

*   *   *

In John 1:42, Jesus looks at Simon, "sees" his apostolic future, and names him Cephas—the Rock. Five verses later, Jesus "sees" Nathanael under the fig tree. That simple revelation completely mystifies Nathanael, and it's clear that the Lord's supernatural knowledge generates faith in the first disciples.

In chapter 2, verse 25, John says that "Jesus knew men so well, that He needed no evidence from others about anyone, for He himself could tell what was in a man's heart." We could cross-reference this verse with 1 Corinthians 14:25: "The prophet ... lays bare the secrets of the heart...." This *knowing* is a function of the prophetic, such that the secrets of the heart have been revealed. For those serving on the ministry team, this knowing rises up time and again. My wife, Janis, was praying for a man, and in her mind's eye saw a pocket calculator. As she asked the Lord for further revelation, the words formed as she prayed for the man: "The Lord has given you a sharp, calculating mind. But if you'll suspend some of your analysis, He'll show you more of His love than you've ever experienced." The gentleman's eyes popped open and he began to laugh. He said that her words were only too true, and received them as the word of the Lord that brought a beautiful gift of freedom and grace.

When the Pharisee Nicodemus comes to Jesus, searching out his heart hungers, Jesus says to him: "In very truth I tell you, no one can see the Kingdom of God unless he has been born again.... Flesh gives birth only to flesh; it is Spirit that gives birth to spirit."[5] The New International and Revised Standard translators capitalized the first "Spirit." That's an interpretation; the more of the Kingdom of God we're born into comes only through the work of the Spirit, capital "S" Spirit, the Spirit of God. We know only too well that it's never *our* good intentions that accomplish anything of the Kingdom.

A few verses later, John the Baptist makes a similar declaration: "One can have only what is given one from heaven." John is talking about spiritual things, and he's speaking to his own disciples. They were feeling a little guilty about the draw Jesus's ministry was exerting, such that people were leaving John to follow Jesus. The Baptist makes that pure declaration of humility: "He must grow greater; I must become less."

John continues: "He who is from the earth belongs to the earth and uses earthly speech. [John is speaking about himself.] He who comes from heaven bears witness to what He has seen and heard." "He whom God sent, He whom God has sent utters the words of God, so measureless is God's gift of the Spirit."[6] What John intends us to hear is the prophetic mandate of the

[5] John 3:3 and 6.
[6] John 3:31 and 34.

42

Lord Jesus, that He is to "bear witness," to "reveal," and all of that "by the Spirit."

*   *   *

The context of chapter 4 is the Lord's encounter with the woman at the well. Verse 24 comes by way of a conclusion to their conversation: "God is Spirit, and those who worship Him must worship in spirit and in truth." Jesus is not teaching so much about who, or what, God is; rather, what He's revealing has to do with relationship: how it is we communicate, interact, connect, with God. We *worship* in "spirit and truth." The issue is spiritual encounter, not this or that form of ritualism, tradition or cultic practice; of holy places, Jerusalem or Gerezim; of a called people, Jewish or Samaritan. It is relationship, loving Heart to loving heart, and that has dynamic consequence.

Verse 29 of chapter 4 makes this clear. After having been with Jesus for a while, the woman declares to her neighbour: "Come and see a man who has told me everything I ever did." The Apostle Paul's description of revelatory ministry in 1 Corinthians 14:25 serves as commentary: Jesus read the "secrets of her heart."

But, she and Jesus had been speaking about some very intimate details of this woman's life, her sex life specifically. In her declaration that He told her "everything she ever did," was she evidencing any shame or condemnation? Tone of voice is everything here. Few of us would brag to our neighbourhoods after treatment that left us feeling humiliated. Nor would we invite them to hear a prophet who would leave them feeling that way. Rather, this woman demonstrated truly evangelistic zeal—she had "good news" to tell. She had no doubt that if her friends and acquaintances would come and meet with Jesus, they would be loved as never before.

* * *

Later in chapter 4, Jesus makes a generic declaration: "For Me it is meat and drink ["bread and butter"] to do the will of Him who sent Me until I have finished the work."[7] Jesus has one mission mandate, one purpose, one goal. In John 5:6, we see how this gets worked out in a practical way. In the NIV, Jesus "learned" that the lame man had been invalided poolside for some time. That seems to imply that Jesus nudged someone and asked, "Who's that guy lying there, and what's his deal?" But that doesn't seem to be the case at all. Rather, here is a specific disclosure: Jesus sees a lame man lying at the poolside, and knowing "the secrets of his heart," He coerces him into health. By way of a working equation, what we see here is that supernatural revelation and sovereign initiative equal miraculous restoration. These three pieces—supernatural revelation, sovereign initiative, and miraculous restoration—are the fulfilment of the will of God, the very reason Jesus was sent.

[7] John 4:34.

* * *

Chapter 5:19 is key in this study of the revelatory ministry of Jesus. Here, He is addressing the accusations brought against Him for healing on the Sabbath. Jesus answers the Pharisees by saying: "The Son can do nothing by Himself; He does only what He sees the Father doing; whatever the Father does, the Son does. The Father loves the Son, and shows Him all that He Himself is doing." This is an amplification of what Jesus said back in John 4:34, that it was "meat and drink to do the will of Him who sent Him." To do only what His Father is doing. Jesus may well be thinking of, or even using, an old parable of a son apprenticing in his father's trade—where a carpenter puts his hand on his son's and guides a chisel as it carves into a piece of wood: "Here, like this ... now you try." Dad wants his son to be a master craftsman, and because of his great love and pride in his boy, he shows him all the tricks of the trade.

In this, let's quickly reflect: have you ever had someone pray for you, only to feel sick inside and wish the person would be quiet and go away? That what he was praying was so far out of line, so far off the mark, that it made you feel worse instead of better? Might it be that person had no mandate for what it was he was praying? That he was conveying his stuff—his best intentions—but it was not mandated by the Father? That instead of master craftsman's work, he was "going against the grain"? If that's the case, we're beginning to fill John 3:6 with some specific content: "Flesh can give birth only to flesh; it is Spirit that gives birth to spirit."

Three chapters later, Jesus says that "it is the Spirit that gives life; ... the words I have spoken to you are both Spirit and life."[8] Five verses later, the disciples witness their recognition and reception of some of what Jesus has revealed—spokesman Peter declares: "Lord, to whom shall we go? Your words are words of eternal life." Loosely paraphrased, Peter is saying, "Lord, You've *ruined* us for business as usual. We can't go back to the way things were." In the following chapter, there is a larger recognition of what Jesus is making known: "How is it that this untrained man has such learning?"[9] In answering their question, Jesus makes crystal clear the revelatory mandate of His ministry: "My teaching is not my own but His who sent Me.... I have not come of My own accord; I was sent by One who is true." As the ministry team moves in this same kind of revelatory authority, men and women touch the Lord's authority of care over their lives, such that they experience life called out of death, hope from torment, peace from despair, freedom from entrapment. As John Wesley said of a woman in one of his meetings: "We besought God on her behalf, and He spoke peace into her soul."

[8] John 6:63.
[9] John 7:16.

*   *   *

In terms of this outpouring of the Spirit, very few who have been touched by the grace of God do not have chapter 7, verses 37, 38, and 39, underlined: "If anyone is thirsty, let him come and drink. Whoever believes in Me, as Scripture says, 'Streams of living water shall flow out from within.' He was speaking of the Spirit which believers in Him would later receive; for the Spirit had not been given, because Jesus had not yet been glorified."

To appreciate fully what Jesus is saying here, we have to understand what "festival" He's talking about in verse 37. Earlier in the chapter, verse 2, John tells his readers that the action is taking place just before the Feast of Tabernacles. We read of this feast in Deuteronomy 16:13. It is the harvest festival, a celebration of all the blessings which the Lord gives; Israel is instructed "to keep the feast with joy" (v. 15).

Since the feast was observed year after year, it became the occasion when prayers for rain were made; if rain came at this time, then a rich harvest could be expected the following season.

All of this was symbolized during the feast as the officiating priest filled a golden pitcher with water, while the choir recited Isaiah 12:3: "With joy you will draw water from the wells of salvation."[10]

---

[10] Raymond Brown, "*The Gospel According to John,*" Vol. 29, in *The Anchor Bible* (New York, Doubleday, 1966) p. 327.

With this as context, we can understand that Jesus's invitation would have caused His hearers to do a double take: He's suggesting that their prayers for water might get answered in ways they did not expect!

*   *   *

In the midst of conflict and confrontation over the nature of Jesus's ministry, the Lord again declares His revelatory mandate: "He who sent Me speaks the truth, and what I heard from Him I report to the world.... I do nothing on My own authority, but in all I say, I have been taught by My Father. He who sent Me is present with Me, and has not left Me on My own.... I tell you what I have seen in My Father's presence.... He who has God for His Father listens to the words of God."[11]

We've been dealing mostly with the auditory, the revelation of the words of God, what God speaks; as we move into chapter 9, Jesus is declared as visual revelation: He is "the light of the world," illuminating and driving back the darkness of life. All of chapter 9, the healing of the man born blind, has to do with "seeing and believing."

Chapter 11 makes the power of the prophetic revelation even more comprehensive, as the resurrecting purposes of God are declared. Lazarus has fallen ill, and Jesus is notified: "When Jesus heard the news, He said, This illness is not to end in death; through it God's glory is to be revealed."[12] There is no question

[11] John 8:28, 38, 42, 47.
[12] John 11:4.

that Lazarus died; the text makes it graphically clear. In verse 39, Martha warns Jesus of the corpse's stench.

Back in verse 4, Jesus said: "This illness is not to end in death." Did Jesus get it wrong, or was He working from a larger revelation—a prophetic mandate, such that God's glory would be revealed? The chapter ends with Lazarus' resurrection. "Loose him, and let him go."

In terms of ministry, it is imperative to note that it is the Lord's to resurrect and the church's to release. My own testimony through this outpouring fits here: I feel like a dead man raised up by the Lord, and let loose by the church at Airport Vineyard. It's something we've seen repeatedly. A woman named Loraine, from Sydney, Australia, was raised up at the prophetic conference the Airport Vineyard hosted in November 1994. On her return home, Loraine's friends, family, and co-workers described her as "a different woman." From a very efficient administrative secretary, she has moved into the training of her church's ministry team, now passionate in this work of the Spirit. Further, in March of 1995, her church hosted a conference at which Larry Randolph, my wife, and I served. Larry's is a prophetic ministry; one meeting he prophesied over this particular woman, calling forth further release of giftings, especially gifts of healing, signs, and wonders, deposited long ago but dormant. Then he turned to the pastoral team and said, "Girls, girls, girls, girls. Get ready, church, for lots of girls." Janis and I looked at each other and knew that this was not in the natural—baby girls, infant female types, but a raising up of women, *young* in ministry. Through that prophetic word, a long-reaching release of grace was brought to bear on the church and its leadership. Again, it is the Lord's to raise up, and the church's to loose and let go, to release. (Loraine's testimony and ministry reflections are included in chapter 5.)

* * *

In John 12:49, we have an echo of the Lord's ministry mandate: "I do not speak on My own authority, but the Father who sent Me has Himself commanded Me what to say and how to speak. I know that His commands are eternal life. What the Father has said to Me, therefore— that is what I speak." If we skipped ahead to chapter 15:15, we'd hear the same thing repeated: "I have disclosed to you everything that I heard from My Father." Essentially the same thing is recorded again in chapter 17, verse 8, in the Lord's great prayer for His disciples: "I have taught them what I learned from You...."

But, this revelation is not confined to the earthly ministry of Jesus, two thousand years ago. This brings us to the Paraclete teachings. "Paraclete," is a Greek word that's hard to translate and do justice. "The Helper." "The Advocate." The One "called alongside." Many feel that the best translation is "Another Revealer,"[13] such that the Paraclete, the

---

[13] Raymond Brown, "The Paraclete in the Fourth Gospel," in *New Testament Studies*, 13 (1966–67) p. 115.

Spirit, will reveal the Father just as Jesus revealed the Father during His earthly ministry. He will continue to reveal the Father after Jesus is raised from the dead. James Dunn puts it strikingly when he says "the Paraclete is the presence of Jesus when Jesus is absent."[14]

Running the Paraclete sayings together, Jesus says: "I will ask the Father, and He will give you another Advocate, who will be with you forever—the Spirit of Truth.... The Advocate, the Holy Spirit whom the Father will send in My name, will teach you everything and remind you of all that I have told you." "When the Advocate has come, whom I shall send you from the Father—the Spirit of Truth that issues from the Father—He will bear witness to Me. And you also are My witnesses."

"There is much more that I could say to you, but the burden would be too great for you now. However, when the Spirit of Truth comes, He will guide you into all the truth; for He will not speak on His authority, but will speak only what He hears; and He will make known to you what is to come. He will glorify me, for He will take what is Mine and make it known to you. All that the Father has is Mine, and that is why I said, He will take what is Mine and make it known to you."[15]

What the Apostle John wants us to hear in all of that is the parallel relationship between Jesus and the Spirit.

[14] Brown, p. 128.
[15] John 14:26; 15:26; 16:12.

Both Jesus and the Spirit come from the Father; both are given and sent by the Father; both teach and reveal the Father's purposes to the disciples; both reveal Truth.

John makes the point explicitly that the Spirit is the "other" Paraclete; meaning, Jesus is the first Paraclete, the first Comforter, the first Advocate, the first Helper, the first One to "come alongside," the first Revealer ... and the Spirit is the second. So, by the Spirit, there is an immediate and direct continuity between the believers and Jesus.[16] And because Jesus sends His Spirit, each generation of Christians can be as close to Him as the last generation—or the first! The Spirit is the immediate link. In terms of mission and ministry, the Spirit continues the revelatory work that Jesus initiated. The Spirit will teach us everything, as He guides us in the Truth. He will remind us of all that Jesus taught, and He will make known what is to come. The Spirit's work is inspired reinterpretation and application of the mission and ministry of Jesus, so that we are able to "reveal the Father" as Jesus did.

We hear this echoed yet again in chapter 18, verse 37, where we have the Lord's "purpose statement." Jesus is standing before Pilate, who is trying to figure out what Jesus has done to get Himself into such trouble. Pilate is also trying to figure out how to get himself off the hook with the Jewish leaders. Jesus confounds him with these words: "My task is to bear

---

[16] James G. D. Dunn, *Jesus and the Spirit* (London, SCM Press, 1975) p. 351.

witness to the truth. For this I was born; for this I came into the world, and all who are not deaf to the truth listen to My voice." In response, Pilate asks the ultimate decision question, "What is truth?"

In John's gospel, Jesus's last words from the cross are "It is finished."[17] What the Lord marks is not merely the termination of His life, but its completion and fulfillment. As He offers up His life, Jesus finishes the work His Father gave Him to do.[18] His atoning death is the *ultimate* revelation of God's Grace, and the power of His love.

*　*　*

That brings us, posthaste, to the resurrection appearance in chapter 20, verse 21. The resurrected Lord Jesus greets His disciples and blesses them with the peace of God. *Shalom aleichem.* Shalom is a big blessing. It conveys not only peace, the cessation of hostility, but much more. Shalom has to do with well-being, the fitting together of all the pieces of our puzzle, the healing of the fractures of our lives. Such blessing, from the One raised from the dead, is no casual greeting—especially when tied to the commission and impartation that follows: "As the Father sent Me, so I send you." Jesus then breathes on them and says: "Receive the Holy Spirit." Those who know their Bibles well are intended to hear an overtone, a "retelling" here—back in Genesis 2:7, the

---

[17] John 19:30.
[18] John 17:4.

Lord God fashioned a human being from the dust of the earth and breathed into his nostrils the breath of life, so that he became a living creature. It is as if Jesus is re-creating and reimparting life, the fullness of life—the fullness of resurrected life, as He breathes on the disciples and shares with them His life-giving Spirit.

Jesus then makes a rather outrageous declaration: "If you forgive anyone's sins, they are forgiven; if you pronounce them unforgiven, unforgiven they remain." For most of us, that's unsettling. There is too much there. We understand that it's not up to us to grant ultimate forgiveness; God alone can do this. So how do we understand this pronouncement of Jesus's? With what we have in hand from our study of the revelatory ministry of Jesus, it's clear that what He is calling forth is that the revelation, the knowledge, the experience of forgiveness *are* ours to impart. It's as if Jesus is saying, "The salvation of those around is essentially dependent on the way in which *you* reveal the Father. How else will they know of His love?"

* * *

My Hebrew professor in seminary would fil! the blackboards with rules of grammar. We'd start moaning, "*Roshi, roshi!*" That's Hebrew for "my head, my head." He'd say, "Don't worry; I don't expect you to remember all of this. I just figure that if I throw enough mud at you, some of it will stick."

It is hoped that this study of John's gospel has illustrated at least three things:

1. In isolating the revelatory ministry of Jesus, it is clear that it was fundamental to His ministry mandate. All that He did revealed what He "heard and saw" the Father doing. He revealed nothing more, and nothing less.

2. What the Father revealed in and through Jesus was *life*, the restoration, the re-creation of life. In John chapter 5, the healing of the lame man, there is revealed specific restoration, localized in space and time. This man is released from all that has crippled him. The goal is nothing less than that as we think about mission and evangelism. It must be more than just getting a person's ticket punched for that great bus trip to heaven.

3. Jesus imparts His Spirit to those who would follow Him in order that they continue in this revelatory work, such that those around receive the Father's restoring, releasing, forgiving, re-creating touch. That's what it means to receive "the word of God with power." *El Verbo*.

This kind of revelation is something that continues to surprise and awe me. Some months ago, I was invited to do some Bible teaching. As part of my preparation, I was praying in the Spirit, and asking that the time be used to reveal and release more of the Father's purposes. The focus text that particular teaching time was from 2 Corinthians 5:17: "If anyone is in Christ, there is a new creation...." After the teaching, a man came up, and said he'd never realized how much that single verse contained. We chatted, and then, out of the blue, one of the many verses I'd just cited in the teaching time rose up within me, from Ephesians, chapter 2. I said to the gentleman, "When you and your wife call Christ to be your peacemaker, and you ask Him to take down the dividing wall between you, brick by brick, then you'll know more of the new creation God wants to work in your life." The way that came out rather surprised me; the guy standing before me was a little shocked too. After a moment he said, "I've been seeing a marriage counsellor for some time, what you just said in twelve seconds makes more sense than the last two years of therapy." This is the pastoral consequence of John 3:6, because it's not our stuff—our insights, intuitions, well-wishing, or even our deepest heartfelt desires for another person's well-being that we're called to impart. Prophetic ministry is the conveying, the "conduiting" of the Father's life-creating verb, what we've seen and heard in the Father's presence, what the Spirit has revealed to us, for the other, that they might receive "one blessing after another."

Pastor Ian Ross for instance, was praying for a woman, and as he asked for revelation, he felt the Lord say that He had a personally tailored love message just for her. As he spoke that to the woman, she seemed overjoyed that God cared that much for her. She opened her eyes and told him that her name was Taylor, and that God had spoken directly and personally to her heart. Another time, the Spirit moved Ian to tell another woman he was praying for that God wanted to write His love message on her heart. Deeply touched, she started to cry. She said later that she was a professional writer, and that the word ministered to her in a unique and personal way.

In this outpouring of God's Spirit, the grace of God breaks over our lives, like "waves of liquid love."[19] Grace upon grace untangles and unties our knots, releases the bits that are stuck, lets us loose, and saturates our very beings, so that we become more and more like Christ, and move in the power and authority that He imparts, such that we build one another up and take His grace to a broken and fractured world.

* * *

After I had taught along these lines, someone stood at the question time and said, "This is all well and good, doing nothing but what you hear the Father authorizing, but what do you do when God isn't speaking?"

That's such an important question, and one that has troubled, even tormented, believers down the centuries. The Greek and Russian Orthodox theologians have been of particular help to me as I've agonized over the felt silence of God: I return to a little book by Anthony Bloom repeatedly. In it he says that often silence is a manifestation of God's mercy; were He to speak, it would be a word of judgement.[20]

While there is great and humbling wisdom in

[19] Charles G. Finney, *Memoirs* (New York, Flemming H. Revell Co., 1876) p. 201.
[20] Anthony Bloom, *Beginning to Pray* (New York, Paulist Press, 1971).

Bloom's insights, it's not always the case. One night I prayed for several people. I turned, and there was man I knew. Because of our upbringings and backgrounds, our personality types and dispositions, we were as different as chalk and cheese. Over the years, our relationship was marked by love and hardship. There were misunderstandings and some judgements both ways, as well as disappointments, unmet expectations, again both ways. I looked him in the eye, and asked, "May I pray for you?" He felt my love and nodded. I put one hand on his shoulder, and another lightly on his forehead, and blessed him in the name of the Lord. No other words of prayer rose up in me; what I found myself doing was gently drawing him in and hugging him. He put his arms around me, buried his face in my shoulder, and wept. We stayed that way for twenty minutes, maybe half an hour.

That whole time, I had almost nothing—no words—to pray. I've been at this long enough to be able to rest in that—the Spirit's work within me has cut loose a lot of striving—I was able to wait knowing that it is the Lord's "responsibility" to bless my friend, not mine. Especially in situations like the one I found myself in, I knew that the Lord's love for him was far greater than mine ever could be.

I prayed silently in the Spirit, and at the end of that time, my friend squeezed me, and then we talked for a bit. I felt really heavy and said I needed to sit down.

My friend has been beaten up pretty badly by the last couple of churches he's served; he's also had the stuffing kicked out of him on the home front too. He came to the meeting that night saying, "God, I need to know Your love, Your unconditional love." When he told me that, I understood why I felt so weighty and why I didn't get any words—that would have only messed up what the Lord was authorizing for him. We talked and prayed a bit more, and I told him of a picture I saw while praying for him. It was of a dairy farm. Jesus was outside the fenced barnyard, calling my friend out to play. I saw that the man for whom I'd been praying couldn't respond; he felt compelled to complete his chores. But Jesus wanted him to play, not so much for my friend's sake, but because Jesus wanted to play with him. When I relayed this picture, my friend looked at me, shook his head, and said "one hundred percent."

Again the commission in John 11:44 comes to bear—"Loose him, and let him go"—and as such, can be considered a mandate for the "Toronto Blessing" prayer ministry: by God's grace, thousands have moved from "death" to life. There has come release *from* and release *to*. It can be viewed as a divine exchange. Longstanding fears, despair, resentments, anxieties, anger, and the like are lifted off, and in their place comes a greater love, a deeper joy, a broader peace. In the middle of this divine exchange is the simple prayer "More, Lord." This request is grounded in Luke 11:9–13, and Jesus's instruction that it is the Father's pleasure to give generously good gifts—and ultimately His Holy Spirit—to those who ask.

Sometimes there are some very funny ways we learn these basic gospel truths. At a question and answer time with pastors and leaders, one gentleman asked about empty form and tradition and use of the prayer "More, Lord." God addressed His concerns the next night. The way in which he was being prayed for was "More, Lord!" And the Lord was bouncing him around, shaking loose some long-standing prejudices and fears, and imparting new liberty and peace!

* * *

In his little book *The Necessity of Prayer*, E.M. Bounds writes:

> God's Word is a record of prayer—of praying men and women, and their achievements; of the Divine warrant of prayer, and of the encouragement given to those who pray. No one can read the instances, commands, examples, and multiform statements which concern themselves with prayer, without realizing that the cause of God, and the success of his work in this world, is committed to prayer.[21]

So as to anchor a priority commitment to the work of the Spirit in prayer and put some content into the gap

[21] E. M. Bounds, *The Necessity of Prayer* (Grand Rapids, Mich., Baker Book House) p. 119.

between "More" and fully articulated prophetic ministry, what follows is a romp through the Book of Acts, and a consideration of the early Church's prayers and intercessions and the correlation they have with ministry and mission growth. It is loosely arranged by subject and theme; we'll be bouncing forward and backward a bit.

*   *   *

In Acts 1:14, the followers of Jesus were together, and "with one accord were constantly at prayer." They had a lot to pray about—the betrayal, crucifixion, and resurrection of their Lord and Master; His appearances to them and His instruction over a period of forty days about the Kingdom of God; His promise that they would receive power when the Holy Spirit came upon them, their final commissioning as His witnesses; His glorious ascension. Even a wee portion of that first hand would keep most of us "constant" at prayer for some time!

"It was during this time ..."[22] What time? The time they were together, constant at prayer; during this time, they got some leadership issues settled.

There are three important aspects to be identified here: 1. unity—they prayed with "one accord"; 2. dedication—they were at prayer "constantly"; 3. leadership—it was recognized and honoured. In one accord, constant at prayer, and under the authority of

[22] Acts 1:15.

care of an anointed leadership, it is not coincidental timing and circumstance that just a few days later the Holy Spirit comes on them with power, such that Peter preaches his first sermon and three thousand come under conviction. Nor is it coincidence that "they meet constantly to hear the apostles teach and to share the common life, to break bread, and to pray." Neither is it a fluke that "a sense of awe was felt by everyone, and many signs and wonders were brought about by the apostles, or that "they enjoyed the favour of the people, and day by day the Lord added new converts to their number." All of this is the substance of Acts chapter 2.

The hours and places of prayer need consideration. "One day at three in the afternoon, the hour of prayer, Peter and John were on their way to the temple."[23] Subsequently, a lame man gets healed, and Peter and John get arrested. In his defence, Peter makes this declaration in verse 16: "The name of Jesus has given strength to this man whom you see and know, and this faith has made him completely well as you can all see." Wanting the focus of things to stay on the "fruit," Peter may well have elbowed the guy in the ribs and whispered, "Jump up and down again!"

Seven chapters later is the story of the conversion of Cornelius, the gentile Centurion; it has a larger significance than just for Cornelius and his family.[24] In it,

[23] Acts 3:1.
[24] Acts 10:24.

Peter is compelled to perceive that what he understood as the way in which God works was too small, too limiting; the vision of the unclean animals in the sheet drove Peter to understand that the Lord had large, redemptive purposes other than for just Israel. He concludes: "I now understand how true it is that God has no favourites."[25] This is how it happened: while observing the hours of prayer, Cornelius receives an angelic visitation about a meeting with Peter. Peter likewise has a vision—the thing is, he falls asleep while he's "observing" the hours of prayer! Cornelius and Peter get together, and because of what has been supernaturally revealed to them, longstanding, traditional barriers of race and religion come down; the Holy Spirit comes on them such that they have a mini-Pentecost, and Cornelius and his household are baptized then and there.

In chapter 16, verse 13, we read that Paul and his associates make their way to a place of prayer, probably a roadside shrine, and there they are able to share the good news of Jesus with a woman named Lydia. That, because "the Lord opened her heart to respond."[26] It seems that Luke, the author of the Acts of the Apostles, would have us mark the connection between prayer, seeking, openness, grace, and the end result, conversion.

But we can never ever bring scientific analysis to

[25] Acts 10:34.
[26] Acts 16:14.

bear on religious experience, such that we could be so self-assured as to conclude—22 percent prayer, 17 percent seeking, 12 percent openness, 49 percent grace = conversion. The best we can do is recognize a correlation, a synergy, a working together.

It's virtually the same cycle with a twist in the verses that follow.[27] In a place of prayer, there is, instead of a searcher, one who suffers spiritual distortion—a girl demonized by a spirit of divination. The "ministry team" here in Acts 16 cut the young woman some slack, all the while exercising their spiritual discernment and testing the spirits. The shouting that she's manifesting. "These men come in the name of the Most High God." It *sounds* orthodox enough, but something is twisted. Paul takes his spiritual authority in Christ; for the woman there comes deliverance in the name of Jesus; for the Apostles, arrest. Paul and Silas end up in jail for "disturbing the peace." Funny how things work out sometimes, isn't it?

And it's marvellous how God redeems things. In verse 25 of chapter 16, Paul and Silas are in prayer, even though it's midnight. They're singing praise to God. That little word "to" is key, for in terms of our worship and the power and presence of the Spirit of God, there's a world of difference between singing "about" God in proclamation and lifting our prayers and praise "to" God in worship.

[27] Acts 16:16.

It's helpful to open this up for a moment. One of the questions I'm asked frequently at the pastors' and leaders' question and answer time has to do with the prayer base of the "Toronto Blessing." Historically, a strong move of intercession has typically preceded an outpouring of God's Spirit. It hasn't caused it; awakening, renewal, and revival are always sovereign grace; but prayer can be considered as preparing and readying a people, even a nation, for a gracious impartation. (Can you think of anything better to do while waiting, especially in light of our considerations of John 3:6?)

This current move of God is no exception, but it has a slight difference. We've sung our confessions, praise and adoration, our petitions and intercessions. Since I'm most familiar with Vineyard music, the following illustrates some of the prayers that we've been singing for some time now. Brian Doerksen's songs "Refiner's Fire" and "No Other Gods" have called us to personal purity of heart. We've cried out our corporate intercessions as we've sung Kevin Prosch's "Save Us Oh God":

"We confess the sins of our nation,
And Lord we are guilty of a prayerless life
We've turned our hearts away from Your laws
And taken for granted Your unchanging grace....
Turn away this curse from our country ...
Open wide the floodgates of heaven ...
Save us oh God
Cleanse us from our unfaithfulness

Let the place where we live be called a place of prayer.

Again, sung directly to God, is Prosch's "So Come":

You have taken the precious
from the worthless
And given us beauty for ashes,
love for hate
You have chosen the weak things of the world
To shame that which is strong to shame the wise
You are help to the helpless,
strength to the stranger
And a Father to the child that's left alone.
And the thirsty You've invited
to come to waters
And those who have no money
come and buy ...
So, Come ...
For You will rend the heavens and
fill Your house with glory....[28]

Building on the last line's petition, David Ruis's song, "Let Your Glory Fall," stands as one of the front pieces to this book because his song has served the "Toronto Blessing" from the first days. As the months have unfolded, the Lord has so graciously let His glory fall not only on a small industrial warehouse at the end of

---

[28] Kevin Prosch, 7th Time, used by permission.

an airport runway, but has sent it forth, literally, to the nations.

These few songs of intercession are but a tiny sample of Vineyard music; the works of other contemporary songwriters could easily be multiplied. Returning to Acts 16:25, where Paul and Silas are singing their praise to God, the text says that "the other prisoners were listening." What it doesn't say is whether they were sympathetic. It may well have been that they were mocking and scoffing—perhaps the jailer was taking the lead in the derision; or it may have been that there was such power and presence in their worship that it exerted a certain draw. What is clear is that the earth starts to shake, the doors burst open, the prisoners' chains fall off, and their jailer figures he's in big trouble. But before things get messy, Paul takes command of the situation. This poor jailer is really rattled, and asks what he must do to be saved. Paul says he's to put his trust in the Lord Jesus, and he and his whole household are baptized.

Before we move on to consider another theme running through the Book of Acts, there are a few conclusions to be drawn loosely. First, there is an inseparable connection between disciplined prayer—prayer at set times, in set places—and the release of God's power, His saving grace, and mercy, and conversion, not just of single individuals, but of households and social networks.

Second, there is a similarly inseparable connection between the disciplines of prayer and fasting and "the presence and power of the kingdom of God. In chapter 13, verses 2–3, there is a convention of prophets and teachers in Antioch. Three items seem to be on the agenda: worship, fasting, and prayer. Out of this consecrated time, there comes a declaration, not just a prophetic word, but a declaration from the Holy Spirit, that Paul and Barnabas are to be set apart and sent off to do some church planting. The next couple of chapters describe their work, and there is this summary statement in Acts 14:3: "Paul and Silas stayed on for some time, and spoke boldly and openly in reliance on the Lord, who confirmed the message of His grace by enabling them to work signs and wonders." This summary statement needs to be held alongside our church growth studies, community demographics, five-year plans, mission philosophies, strategic initiatives, and seeker sensitivity—worship, fasting, and prayer are the power impetus to church growth.

Towards the end of chapter 14, Paul and Silas return to Antioch; their "quarterly achievements report" is due. They tell their stories and bring this word: "To enter the Kingdom of God we must undergo many hardships." They appoint elders and, with further prayer and fasting, commit them to the Lord—again a clear signal that this work is a spiritual enterprise. Jesus's word in John 15:5 resounds here: "Apart from Me you can do nothing." Were it not for their continuous intercessions in the Spirit, the Apostles would have accomplished very little in terms of Kingdom ministry.

*   *   *

Another correlation to be recovered from this study of Acts is the connection between prayer and mission.

After Peter and John's first release from prison, the early Church meets with one accord; they gather for prayer. There is praise and adoration as God's sovereignty is declared, then this supplication: "Now, O Lord, enable those who serve you to speak Your word with all boldness. Stretch out Your hand to heal and cause signs and wonders to be done through the name of Your holy servant Jesus."[29]

It serves us well to do some evaluation here. Was that a prayer that was pleasing to God? Did it give expression to His will and purpose? Was it worthy of being asked "in the name of Jesus"? The next verses tell the tale: "When they had ended their prayer, the building where they were assembled rocked, and all were filled with the Holy Spirit and spoke the word of God with boldness." It seems abundantly clear that God not only heard and answered their prayers, but that what they asked for was exactly what God desired to give.

In this account there is another dynamic implicity at work: empowerment for ministry is the practical end for which the Spirit is given. Unpacking the text makes this clear. At the start of Acts chapter 4, Peter and John were "engaged in ministry." These were the "anointed men of God," the ones who had been closest to the Lord Jesus. But in verse 24 of the same chapter, the gathered believers prayed with one voice, and in verse 32 *all* were filled with the Holy Spirit

[29] Acts 4:23–30.

and spoke the word of God with boldness. The mission and ministry of the church is not only the work of those who have "high profile," the "inner circle"; rather, all those who are filled with Christ's Spirit have powerful anointing to tell out the gospel. The balance of the Book of Acts is testimony after testimony to this very fact—we read account after account of the mighty word and work of God, how it changes people's lives and brings wholeness, freedom, peace, grace.

This inclusive experience of ministry is declared on the forefront of Peter's Pentecost sermon in chapter 2. There he quotes the Old Testament prophet Joel, stating: "God says, In the last days I will pour out my Spirit on all people; and your sons and daughters shall prophesy; your young men shall see visions, and your old men shall dream dreams. Yes, even on My servants, both men and women, I will pour out My Spirit, and they shall prophesy."[30] What Peter teaches here is that the Spirit of Christ is poured out on "all flesh," not only on the privileged few, the "spiritual giants," but also on the non-privileged—not only on the sons, but the daughters too, not only on the old and wise, but also the young; not only the masters, but also the menservants and the maids. By implication, he speaks of himself, an unlearned, unprivileged Galilean fisherman, now graced and empowered for ministry; by extrapolation, we can include ourselves, however we see our status in life,

[30] Acts 2:17–18

because in Christ we are graced and empowered for ministry to "speak the word of God with all boldness."

We read more on prayer and mission in Acts 6:4. There the Apostles delegate various ministry concerns, and as the teachers and administrators, they name their top priority: "prayer and the ministry of the word." The next few verses have to do with commissioning, as others join in the work: these newly appointed ministers are prayed for with the laying on of hands, and as the various aspects of ministry are covered through a variety of involvements and responsibilities, "the word of God spread more and more widely; the number of disciples [N.B. *disciples*, not just believers, but those who have been nurtured to some maturity] increased rapidly."

With home base covered, Peter and John are released as itinerants and head off to Samaria. A dramatic move of God has taken place there, "outside" the confines of Jerusalem—a beginning to the fulfilment of the mission mandate named back in Acts 1:8: "... Jerusalem, Judea, Samaria, and the farthest corners...." These "outsiders" have confessed in the Lord Jesus Christ; they've been baptized in His name. Peter and John lay their hands on these new converts and impart to them the Holy Spirit.

* * *

Back in Jerusalem, the first Christian martyr, Stephen, cries out as he is dying, "Lord Jesus, receive my Spirit."[31] He also prays for blessing and release: "Lord,

[31] Acts 7:59.

do not hold this sin against them." What has that to do with mission? A man named Saul was standing by holding everybody's cloaks—stoning is sweaty work. There is "guilt by association"—but from it Saul—soon to become the Apostle Paul—is released, and as St. Augustine put it: "If Stephen had not prayed, the Church would not have had Paul."

In his call and conversion, Saul gets knocked off his "high horse," and the risen Lord Jesus has a few things to say to him.[32] Concurrently, Ananias receives a vision; he's to go to a particular place and ask for a man named Saul. Ananias will find the man "at prayer." That's a marvellous understatement—Saul had been persecuting the followers of Jesus Christ; he had stood by as Stephen was stoned. The risen Lord Jesus appears to him and asks why Saul is persecuting Him; he's struck blind and told to wait for someone to come and talk to him. Again, if all that happened to you, wouldn't you be at prayer? Prayers of repentance, at the very least!

Ananias obeys the Spirit's promptings, and when he finds Saul, he gently lays his hands on him and says, "My brother Saul ..." There is such a tender declaration of the grace of the Lord in Ananias's words—such love and acceptance and forgiveness. "My brother Saul, the Lord Jesus, who has appeared to you on your way here, has sent me to you so that you may recover your sight and be filled with the

[32] Acts 9:11.

Holy Spirit."[33] Paul's spiritual growth curve goes straight up.

All of that because Ananias acted on what he had received. It boggles the mind how different things might have been if, instead of obeying the vision, he had written it off and over his cornflakes simply mumbled something to his wife about the terrible dream he'd had the night before.

*   *   *

Ananias and Paul were not the only ones to have received visions. Peter's and Cornelius's have already been named. Paul received a vision that changed the course of his ministry direction and focus.[34] He and his ministry team found themselves "prevented" from going to Asia. One can only read between the lines; it seems that there was strong inner conviction that would not "allow" them to proceed. Later, they were "convinced" that they should go to Macedonia. This kind of internal motivation necessarily sounds off the wall to those not familiar with attending to the direction the Spirit gives, but in this season of outpouring, similar stories of directional leadings, to go or to stay, have remarkable similarity to this witness in Acts 16.[35]

In Acts 21:10, a man named Agabus prophesies over Paul and tells out some of what the future holds

---

[33] Acts 9:17.
[34] Acts 16:6, 7, 9, and 10.
[35] See also Acts 21:4, "warned by the Spirit...."

for the Apostle. He misses it on a couple of accounts in terms of detail, but the Apostle is "built up" nonetheless. In the following chapter, Paul receives further direction through a vision that comes during a time of prayer.[36] Paul also receives revelatory encouragement during his times in jail: the Lord appears to him and reveals the next few steps of what's about to unfold.[37] Similarly, in Acts 27:23, during a time of high stress, "words" are given that bring comfort and assurance, and that declare God's sovereignty and providential care.

Through the ministry teams of the "Toronto Blessing," unnumbered believers have been met by the Lord and received similar words of assurance, comfort, encouragement. These have made a world of difference in their lives, for with the word has come a release of resource that has not only sustained in difficult times, but also brought about a new future and a hope that did not exist before.

* * *

There is in the Book of Acts clear witness to the inseparable connection between prayer and ministry. In the extreme, there's the case in Acts 9:40. A disciple named Tabitha falls ill and dies. Peter is called. He kneels beside her body, prays, calls the corpse by name, and helps her to her feet. Paul does essentially

[36] Acts 22:17.
[37] Acts 23:11.

the same thing in raising Eutychus from the dead in chapter 20. And in the last chapter of Acts, we read of the connection between prayer and healing.

* * *

One last observation. There are at least five significant occasions in the Book of Acts where prayer is not explicitly named. Held really loosely, it seems that Luke is inferring something about the fundamental dynamisms of life in Christ: in chapter 5 there is no mention of prayer—and Ananias and Sapphira drop dead. In chapter 7 there is no prayer; Stephen gets arrested and tries to convert the high priest. He gives a religious history lesson, telling out God's faithfulness, but those to whom he is preaching are described as being "heathen at heart" and deaf to the truth. While there is no positive response to the gospel, there is a particularly negative reaction to the preacher. In chapter 15, there's nothing of prayer. In that chapter the dynamic duo Paul and Barnabas suffer such irreconcilable differences that they split up and go their separate ways. In chapter 17, no prayer. Paul preaches at the Areopagus, and instead of knocking it out of the park the way he used to, he dribbles out a single. In chapters 24 and 25, no mention of prayer. Paul tries to argue his case before governor Felix and King Agrippa, unsuccessfully.

If we read between the lines and hold it in tension with what we've been tracing—if we paint in big, broad strokes—the case may be made that Luke is telling us that the Church's health, unity, and the power for proclamation *depend* on the prayers and intercessions of God's people.

We have isolated some of the larger themes and dynamics that are key to our life in Christ and the mission we're called to: issues of unity, leadership, spiritual outpouring and empowerment, proclamation, healing, spiritual discernment and deliverance, visions and prophetic declaration and direction, commission and call. As we've given consideration to the place prayer played in the life of the early Church, we have traced issues of spiritual discipline, the release of spiritual power, the taking down of walls that separate us from one another, and the proclamation of the gospel in the knowledge that Jesus has called His followers to "open eyes that are blind, to turn those who are in darkness towards the light, from the dominion of Satan to God, so that they may obtain forgiveness of sins and a place among those whom God has made His own."[37]

* * *

Pray with Fire is subtitled *Interceding in the Spirit*. The question that generates this study is, "How do we pray in the midst of revival?" And that generates a further question—"How do we respond to and work with the Spirit?"

As our study of John's gospel demonstrates, the Spirit reveals; receiving the Holy Spirit, believers are

[38] Acts 26:18.

sent out to reveal God's gracious love just as Jesus did during His earthly ministry.[39] As Luke describes things in his account of the Acts of the Apostles, it is prayer that undergirds, sustains, and empowers the life of the early Church.

In taking things further, we look to the Apostle Paul to walk out some specifics within the local gatherings of believers. In his writings, we trace dynamic process: the transformation of life, both personal and corporate, *in the midst of the ongoing outpouring of Christ's Spirit.* As personal letters, Paul's writings serve as practical counsel within specific contexts, and typically, Paul writes his letters on a corrective basis. Rarely is he initiating; usually he is responding to concerns and difficulties that have arisen within the local fellowships. By purpose and intent, then, Paul characteristically is giving counsel and direction to issues of excess, pride, elitism, disorder, negligence, control, deception, and suppression. Given this current move of God, we discover a striking similarity to the concerns that are generated by friends and antagonists!

Recognizing the extent and scope of Paul's writings, we are faced with the question of how to proceed. Rather than listing and commenting on the relevant passages of Scripture as they appear chronologically in our Bibles, we will consider some of the Apostle's several themes and subjects. Those seeking a more

---

[39] John 20:21.

detailed commentary are referred to Gordon Fee's *God's Empowering Presence: The Holy Spirit in the Letters of Paul.*[40]

Fee declares his bias early in his introduction:

> I am convinced that the Spirit in Paul's experience and theology was always thought of in terms of the personal presence of God. The Spirit is God's way of being present, powerfully present, in our lives and communities as we await the consummation of the Kingdom of God. Precisely because he understood the Spirit as God's personal presence, Paul also understood the Spirit always in terms of an empowering presence; whatever else, for Paul the Spirit was an *experienced* reality.[41]

He is not alone is this conviction. N. T. Wright states: "Paul's doctrine of the Spirit is far more central and characteristic than his doctrine of justification by faith."[42] Writing on the community life of the early Church, James Dunn notes two striking features: one, their exuberance and joy; and two, their sense of the numinous, the presence and power of the Spirit of God. With biting understatement, Dunn declares:

[40] Gordon Fee, *God's Empowering Presence: The Holy Spirit in the Letters of Paul* (Peabody, Mass., Hendrickson Pub., 1994).
[41] Fee, p. xxi.
[42] N. T. Wright, *The Interpretation of the New Testament 1861–1986* (Oxford, Oxford University Press, 1988) p. 203.

"These were not simply social get-togethers marked by cheerful camaraderie. They were conscious of the eschatological Spirit, the power of God in their midst."[43] Ernst Kasemann, in his chapter on worship in the early Church, states that "experience of the Spirit is the real hall-mark of post-Easter Christianity.... The [early Church] viewed *pneuma* [the Spirit] as the power of ecstasy and miracle."[44]

*   *   *

For Paul, the Spirit is not merely a doctrinal or credal concept, but Holy Activity; He—not "It"—is spoken of in terms of power agency. As if turning a precious diamond, the Apostle considers facet after facet of his pneumatology: the Spirit is giver of life, sanctifier, revealer, persuader, baptizer, unifier, and helper. By the Spirit, believers are adopted, justified, led, filled, and sanctified; in the Holy Spirit is Kingdom righteousness, peace, and joy. Through the Spirit, God's love floods our hearts and brings new life to our mortal bodies. The church is gifted with the charismatic graces for ministry through the Holy Spirit; He is the enabler in prophecy, prayer, and speaking in tongues.

The Spirit searches all things, knows and reveals the mind of God, teaches the gospel to believers, dwells within us, accomplishes all things, bears witness, redirects our desires, intercedes, and works all things together.

[43] Dunn, p. 188.
[44] Ernst Kasemann, *Perspectives on Paul* (London, SCM Press, 1969) p. 122.

In all of this, Paul understands that the reception and appropriation of the Spirit is an ongoing impartation. Having "received" the Spirit at conversion, we now "live" by the Spirit, for the Spirit "dwells" within us.[45] We are literally "being led by the Spirit"; the Spirit of adoption "enabling" us to cry *Abba,* Father; the Spirit "affirming" our spirits that we are God's children.[46] Similarly, the Spirit is the "source of our lives" and "directs our course"; Paul admonishes that we are to "sow the Spirit."[47] Grammatically, he uses present participles—"in *giving* His Spirit"[48]—rather than the aorist, past tense, complete—"He *gave* us His Spirit." Like John 1:16, this implies furthering bestowal, "one blessing after another." Paul uses the present tense in Galatians 3:5, "when God gives you the Spirit and works miracles among you," because in Galatians especially, his instruction follows experiential lines: the question he is addressing in the letter is, having received the Spirit by faith, how does one then live?

In Ephesians 5:18, Paul's "do not be drunk with wine but let the Spirit fill you" admonition is perfectly balanced syntax. His "never do so" parallels

[45] Romans 8:9. *Este, oikei, elabete, summarturei* are all active, indicative, present verb forms, implying linear, continuous action.
[46] Romans 8:14–15.
[47] Galatians 5:18 and 25; 6:8.
[48] 1 Thessalonians 4.8, *didonta*; here the gifting of the Spirit is given unto a life of greater and greater holiness and purity. Contrast Romans 5.5, *dothentos*, "given to us," and 2 Corinthians 1.22 and 5.5, *dous*, where the references harken back to conversion, hence the aorist tense.

"always be so"—and the emphasis is not so much on the contrast between intoxication and inspiration as it is on the continuous filling of the Holy Spirit, such that the characteristics of community life together are as obvious in the Ephesians' church as the effects of too much wine are obvious in the other.[49]

Further, the Spirit knows and reveals all things— the "depths of God" (1 Corinthians 2:11) and the deep groanings of the believer's heart (Romans 8:26) and the secrets of the hearts of those who do not believe (1 Corinthians 14:25). His revelation is never shaming exposure, but rather disclosure that stirs and prompts conviction, and with it, there is imparted the grace of God such that gospel salvation comes through Christ. In this, Paul is insistent that the Spirit plays the decisive role in our life in Christ, from the awakening of faith, to the forming of more of Christ in our everyday lives, through to our ultimate and final glorification in our Lord.

To this end, he prays for ongoing revelation, wisdom, and understanding, such that we can know God more fully; as we know His heart for us, hope, confidence, and freedom will rise within us as we receive yet further giftings of the Spirit's power that brings ever-greater fulfilling of our lives in Christ.[50]

---

[49] Fee, p. 721.
[50] Ephesians 1:17–23.

Four times in his letters, the Apostle uses the phrase "the power of the Holy Spirit."[51] He regularly joins "power" and "Spirit" in such a way that the presence of the Spirit is equated with the presence of God's power.[52] Ephesians 3:16 can be considered a representative text: there Paul prays that God would grant "inner strength and power through His Spirit." This is not raw power; it is manifested with express purpose—that believers would know more of Christ's immeasurable love for us, that we would become "filled with the very fullness of God." This distinction is an imperative one; the Apostle Peter faced it while in Samaria. After watching Peter and John lay hands on the new converts and impart to them the Holy Spirit, the magician Simon offered money to the Apostles, saying, "Give me the same power, so that anyone I lay my hands on will receive the Holy Spirit."[53] Not dissimilarly, while ministering in Helsinki, a pastor asked me to pray for an increase of power in his life. That is not an uncommon request, but with this particular gentleman, it did not sit right. As I prayed silently for him for a while, I had the strong sense that the request was more for his glory than for God's, that an increase in power would increase his little kingdom, not the Lord's. He didn't look too happy as I prayed for a filling of the power

[51] Romans 15:13 and 19; 1 Thessalonians 1:5; Galatians 4:29.
[52] 1 Corinthians 2:4; Galatians 3:5; Romans 1:4; Ephesians 3:16; 2 Timothy 1:7.
[53] Acts 8:14–19

of God's *love* in his life, that he be released with a new freedom and authority to serve, to give his life that others might live.

In Ephesians 3:20, things are nuanced yet again, for Paul commits the Church "to the One who has power," *dunamenoe*. The Apostle is reframing his earlier prayer, that the Spirit would strengthen the believers in Ephesus in their innermost selves so that Christ would dwell in their hearts in love.

The essence of this prayer is the substance of the Apostle's counsel to his young friend Timothy. Paul reminds him three times to rely on the Spirit's power.[54] This is not just "nostalgic remembering," but rather, by stepping into and living out the directives received prophetically, Timothy will "fan into flame" the gifts, anointing, and ministry he received in the Spirit. This is precisely the issue in 2 Timothy 1:7, where Paul admonishes his friend: "The Spirit that God gave us is no cowardly spirit, but one to inspire power, love, and self-discipline." God has poured out His Spirit on the likes of men and women like Timothy, like us; especially in this current outpouring, we understand that what this means is that there is no place for cowardice, intimidation, or spiritual insecurity; this is not a time for timidity. The order of the day is Holy boldness, power, love, and personal accountability. As we soak in the grace of God, and

[54] 1 Timothy 1:18, 4:14 and 2 Timothy 1:6–7.
  Ephesians 6:19.

the Spirit forms more and more of Jesus in us, we understand that we find ourselves, not at the end of the process, but in the middle. Our receiving of the Spirit is for a giving; our coming to special meetings is for a going. We keep only what we give away. We pray "in the power of the Spirit" in order to "boldly and freely make known the mystery of the gospel."

* * *

For thousands, this "Toronto Blessed" move of God's Spirit has driven home the conviction that life in Christ is essentially charismatic, that the spiritual dynamisms of the early Church are normative, and not exceptional.

We have already noted the Spirit's present ongoing impartation of grace "works miracles" in the midst of the Church at Galatia.[55] This text, and others, implies that the Spirit continues to do "signs and wonders" such that they are a regular and expected expression of life in the Spirit.[56] Written several years prior, the directives in 1 Thessalonians 5:19–22 stand as the earliest record of the basically charismatic nature of New Testament communities of faith. The evidence from 1 and 2 Thessalonians, as well as the admonition in 1 Corinthians 14:1, "earnestly seek the gifts of the Spirit..." indicates that prophecy was a regular, expected, and nurtured phenomenon in Paul's

[55] Galatians 3:5.
[56] 1 Corinthians 2:4 and 1 Thessalonians 1:5.

churches; 1 Corinthians indicates that speaking in tongues was also a part of the broad experience of Spirit phenomena; and the matter-of-fact listing of charismatic gifts in 1 Corinthians 12:7–11 and Romans 12 demonstrates that the worship of the early Church was far more charismatic than has been true for most of its subsequent history.

Dunn devotes more than fifty pages to his chapter "The Charismatic Spirit—the Consciousness of Grace," and in it he seeks to establish "the fundamental role of experience, not least the experience of grace, in the shaping of Paul's theology."[57] Dunn asserts that the Spirit is the power that operates on a person's *heart*, the "experiential centre," that transforms believers from the inside out.[58] But New Testament spirituality is not just a personal, individualistic experience; Dunn is insistent:

> Fundamental to Christian community is the shared experience of Spirit and grace.... Each individual is a member of the [Body of Christ] only in so far as the Spirit knits him into the corporate unity by the manifestations of grace through him. To have the Spirit is to experience the power of grace constantly seeking to come to concrete expression.59

[57] Dunn, p. 200.
[58] Dunn, p. 201.
[59] Dunn, p. 262.

Historically, theologians and Bible commentators have slighted this fact; Fee comments: "We would prefer to believe that the Pauline churches were more like ours and less like the Pauline and Lukan documents suggest they really were."[60]

* * *

The concerns and problems that Paul sought to address in his letters, both to the Church at Thessalonica and Corinth, serve us well, given the questions and concerns raised by the "Toronto Blessing." The situations that called forth Paul's address were as follows: some within these two communities were less than delighted with the charismatic phenomena manifested within the assemblies. Paul's instruction, reduced to bare minimum, is "adjustment"—but not elimination. Excesses and abuse are noted and corrected. Paul refuses to tame the faith by eliminating what could prove troublesome.

In 1 Thessalonians, the Church is clearly admonished—they are not to "stifle inspiration." The New International Version amplifies the Apostle's instruction: "do not put out the Spirit's fire." The old King James is actually closest to a literal translation: "quench not the Spirit." Within this young Christian community, there were difficulties, excesses, immaturities, and abuses, many of which were generated out of a spiritual zealousness. Paul is

[60] Fee, p. 389.

insistent that the Thessalonians must not quench the Spirit; recognizing that there are problems, he will not let them throw out the baby with the bathwater. But by not quenching or not despising spiritual gifts and freedoms, neither is he suggesting that anything goes in the name of the Spirit. They are to "test all things, holding fast the good and avoiding every evil form."[61] Discernment, however, must not lead to dampening the Spirit's fire or compromising His gifts and the release of ministry that He calls forth and authorizes.

Similarly, in Paul's first letter to the Corinthian church, he has to address an overspiritualized group who were making believe they had arrived. They felt they could speak the language of angels, and so concluded that they had achieved some superior spiritual experience. Again, the purpose of 1 Corinthian 14 is not so much instructional as it is corrective. As he responds to questions and concerns and out and out abuse of tongues and prophecy, Paul categorically refuses to compromise the dynamic power of the Spirit in the midst of a congregation's life together by eliminating what proves troublesome and problematic. He makes it clear that the difficulties lie, not in the Corinthians' giftedness, but in their attitude towards one another, and the ways in which they are abusing the gifts they have received.

[61] 1 Thessalonians 5:20–21.

* * *

Paul's conviction that life in Christ is essentially charismatic rises out of his own experience. He is able to say:
"I am more gifted in tongues than any of you."[62] He
tells, guardedly, of visions and revelations he himself has
experienced; he states that the signs and wonders and
miracles that God worked through him are signals of his
apostolic ministry. If one is allowed to read between the
lines, Paul himself experienced physical healing several
times, given that he'd been flogged within an inch of his
life five times, beaten with rods three times, and given
up for dead once, after having been stoned. In addition,
the course of his ministry was directed by revelation and
prophetic words that seemingly came both privately and
in the course of communal worship.[63]

Further, in the various lists and considerations of the
Spirit's gifts, "prophecy," or the "prophet," is the only
constant throughout.[64] Such a sweep indicates the per-
vasiveness of prophetic ministry in the life of the early
Church. The charism "prophecy" occurs more than
thirty times, in Romans, 1 Corinthians, Ephesians, 1
and 2 Thessalonians, and 1 Timothy. "Tongues," in
contrast, occurs twelve times, and the references are
densely concentrated in 1 Corinthians 12:14.

[62] 1 Corinthians 14:18.
[63] 1 Corinthians 14:18; 2 Corinthians 12:1–4, 12; 2 Corinthians
11:24–25; Galatians 1:12, 2:2; Ephesians 3:3; Acts 13:2.
[64] 1 Thessalonians 5:20; 1 Corinthians 11:4–5; 12:10–14:40; Romans
12:6; Ephesians 2:20; 3.5; 4:11; 1 Timothy 1:18.

In working with one of Paul's prophetic metaphors, an important dynamic is recognized. If in 1 Thessalonians 5:19 the fire of the Spirit can be quenched, so also can it be fanned into flame, as in 2 Timothy 1:6–7. Paul seems to imply a perfect parallelism here: the Spirit's fire is extinguished by stifling prophetic ministry; it is stirred up by nurturing the prophetic word. As Paul understands things, there is *one* way that this is done: the gifts of the Spirit are fanned into flame through mutual prophetic encouragement, especially in context of worship and personal prayer. Add to this the Apostle's directives in 1 Corinthians 14 that prophecy "builds, stimulates and encourages" those in Christ, as well as convicting the hearts of unbelievers.[65]

But because the balance of Paul's writings serve a corrective purpose, there is the implicit recognition that the gifts and the Spirit can be abused within the Christian community. And because of the absolutely dynamic role of the Spirit in an individual's life, as well as the community life of the Church, Paul will not correct abuse by commanding disuse. Rather, the remedy for abuse is proper use.[66] It is for this reason that in 1 Thessalonians 5:19 he begins his exhortations with the general caution "Do not put out the Spirit's fire." He is insistent: the Spirit is manifested, stirred up, and nurtured in the community of faith through the prophetic word.

[65] 1 Corinthians 14:3 and 24.
[66] Fee, p. 59.

* * *

In Paul's experience, the free and spontaneous nature of worship and prayer is orchestrated by the Spirit Himself. So, when he calls the Thessalonians to "rejoice always,"[67] such joyous prayer is the supernatural activity of the Holy Spirit in the community. For Paul, the Spirit's presence and power and our experience of prayer, joy, and praise are inseparably tied together. Similarly, in Colossians 3:16, where Paul calls believers to "sing from the heart with gratitude to God," the focus is not so much on *our* attitude towards God as we sing, but on our awareness of *His* towards us, for it is this awareness that prompts such singing in the first place.[68]

Paul's directive to "rejoice always; again, I say rejoice"[69] places an emphasis on joy that is not so much a perpetual "Don't worry—be happy" bliss, but rather, a joy that clearly has source: believers "rejoice *in the Lord.*" And that, because of Presence: "The Lord is near."[70] The immediate, experiential "closeness" of God is the source of gratitude, freedom, and peace. In Romans 15:13, the Apostle intertwines these very dynamics in his prayer: "May God, who is the ground of hope, fill you with all joy and peace as you lead the life of faith until, by the power of the Holy Spirit, you overflow with hope."

---

[67] 1 Thessalonians 5:16–18.
[68] Fee, p. 655.
[69] Philippians 4:4.
[70] Philippians 4:5.

Without a dynamic understanding and experience of the Spirit's presence and power working in us, the imperatives that Paul issues the churches are pious platitudes that sound elusive if not unobtainable, and leave us feeling like second-class Christians. Rather than lifting failure and guilt, our own attempts at obedience often further our frustrations. But because this gospel joy is a *gift* given by God, the experience of His own powerful presence turns these imperatives to invitations that call us to a fuller appropriation of the very intentions God has for us.

Commenting on Galatians 5:22, and the fruit of the Spirit, Fee asks: "One wonders, does the general lack of joy that characterizes so much of contemporary North American Christianity suggest that the life of the Spirit has been generally downplayed in the interest of a more cerebral or performance-oriented brand of faith?"[71] Those who have been "Toronto Blessed" have found a marked release from competitiveness and performance orientation, both in the conduct of their ministries and the living out of their personal faith. A profound refreshment and rest, a freedom from nervousness and anxiety, and a new measure of peace, joy, and gratitude are more than evident. Those with whom they live, the congregations they serve, unchurched friends, even casual observers are noticing the differences. For instance, an acquaintance of twenty years recently told me that out of curiosity, she had gone to the Airport

[71] Fee, p. 448.

Vineyard. (She is not a regular churchgoer.) We chatted about her experience: she said she really enjoyed the music, and when I asked if she went forward for prayer, she smiled and said she did. I asked what happened. She said, "It was very relaxing."

I had met up with her at a big birthday party; our conversation was then interrupted. Hours later, when I was saying goodbye on my way out, she called to me from across the room: "Guy, God is at work in your church!" I jovially yelled back "How do you know?" She said: "Because I've never seen you look so happy!"

* * *

Foundational to this freedom and release is the immediate revelation of the Father-heart of God. As it is called forth in prayer, it is the language of intimate relationship rather than formal, ritualistic address. Dunn says that for Jesus, "this sense of God was so real, so loving, so compelling, that whenever He turned to God it was the cry 'Abba' that came most naturally to His lips."[72] To call God *Abba* is experiential awareness, not intellectual belief. Recalling John 5:20, "the Father loves the Son ..." the word for love here is *philei*, "delighted friendship love," the felt affection and closeness of a beloved. Jesus knew that the Master and Creator of the Universe was also His Father, under whose authority of care He lived His life. In the face of the growing antagonism and animosity that He was

[70] Dunn, p. 26.

facing, this knowledge left Him in a confident position. That's why, in Matthew 11:29, Jesus instructs His followers to "learn from Him." Previously, in Matthew 11:27, Jesus says that no one knows the Father but the Son, and "those to whom the Son chooses to reveal Him." Dunn amplifies things helpfully here when he says: "To know God is to know Him as Father."[73]

This is the heart of the gospel mission: Jesus's knowledge of God is unparalleled, as John 1:18 makes clear: "No one has ever seen God; God's only Son, He who is nearest to the Father's heart, has made Him known." The very purpose for Jesus's coming was to reveal—and also to impart: "Learn from Me...." This is also the concluding petition Jesus makes in His priestly prayer for His followers: that they—we—would know the same love that the Father had for Jesus—that the love of the Father would be *in* us.[74]

The single greatest distinctive in Jesus's instruction on prayer is that He taught His disciples to pray in the same way as He did. Again, Dunn: "Their use of *Abba* was somehow dependent on their relationship with Jesus; their 'Abba' was *derivative* from Jesus' 'Abba.' "[75] Our son- and daughter-ship originates in Jesus's Sonship; Fee states: "believers now, by the Spirit *of the Son*, are using *the language of the Son*."[76]

---

[73] Dunn, p. 34.
[74] John 17:26.
[75] Dunn, p. 25.
[76] Fee, pp. 411–13.

The Apostle Paul echoes this truth, stating that the *Abba* "cry" in Galatians 4:6–7 is "proof," the evidence of our new relationship with God. This "crying out" suggests spontaneity, a heartfelt freedom and confidence; there is nothing forced or contrived—for in Christ, we are beloved children of God, and no longer slaves or orphans. That the cry comes from our "hearts" implies relational intimacy; Paul insists that "the Spirit of the Son" takes us far beyond mere conformity to religious obligations and formalities, and draws us from curse to blessing.[77] This is the dominating thrust of Paul's argument in his letter to the Galatians, for our spiritual adoption by God is the ultimate expression of grace. In the context of the letter to the Galatians, this is contrasted with Torah obedience, duty, and performance; in Christ, we are not "slaves," but "sons." And by the Spirit of the Son, we are not *only* sons, but "heirs."

Complementing this instruction in Galatians is Paul's teaching in Romans 8:14–17. Following the same lines, the Apostle repeats his argument of adoption and impartation, declaring that our inheritance is nothing short of God's eternal glory.

Lest things get too heady, Paul makes it clear that we live out our inheritance in the midst of suffering. Ours is not unbroken sunshine; this is no problem-free philosophy. Working from Romans 8:17–27, the Apostle is unyielding in his faith: it is *in the midst* of

[77] Galatians 3:13–15.

our very sufferings that the Spirit manifests grace and power. Knowing Christ means knowing both the power of His resurrection and the fellowship of His sufferings.[78] It is in this context, in the midst of our weaknesses, that the Spirit "comes to our aid" as an intercessor on our behalf.

Given whatever present suffering and trials we face, and the larger picture of our life in Christ, we don't know what to pray. The Spirit "steps in" to intercede on our behalf, and as we pray in tongues, what the Spirit "sees" and "reads" in our hearts—these form the substance of our unspoken prayers. When contrasted with 1 Corinthians 14:14–15, where Paul distinguishes "praying in tongues" and "praying with the mind," Romans 8:27, "we do not know what to pray," is unnecessary if the Spirit is only "assisting" us as we form our own feeble prayers. Rather than mindless activity, Paul sees praying in the Spirit as key to the unfolding of God's purposes for us... such that "overwhelming victory is ours through Him who loved us."[79]

In Christ, by His Spirit, we have a future and a hope—an "overflowing hope."[80] Fee is himself exuberant in his comments: "Such future-oriented people live in the present in a way different from the rest ... so confident of the future that they can pour themselves into the present with utter abandon, full of joy

[78] See also Philippians 3:9–10.
[79] Romans 8:37.
[80] Romans 15:13.

and peace, because nothing in the present can ultimately overwhelm them. Such people make the Christian faith a truly attractive alternative."[81] There are some telling witnesses to this very fact in the testimony chapter.

* * *

While Paul leaves much that we might wish he'd elucidated, the Apostle will have this much clear: love is the *only* legitimate end of any and all manifestations of the Spirit's power and presence. The very reason God gives believers gifts is the edification of the Church, which is precisely what love aims at. He begins his corrective instruction in 1 Corinthians 12; again, the difficulty is that some in Corinth were conducting themselves as if their ability to pray in tongues was a demonstration of their spiritual "seniority." In referring to their prayer ability as the "tongues of angels" in chapter 13:1, he is alluding to a hyperspirituality that struts about as having arrived. Paul will not have it. Glossolalia is not directed towards people, for others. Nor is it ecstasy. Rather, Paul teaches out of his own experience, and says that it is directed towards God, the Spirit praying through his spirit, without interference of his own ego. He receives it as graced assistance in his weakness. As such, these prayers in the Spirit are the "pure will of God," because they are the Spirit's intercessions, not his own.

[81] Fee, p. 623.

Tongues are not a signal of high spirituality but God's resource for human inability. Paul gives open recognition to our weaknesses, "climaxed by the glossolalia as a sign of our helplessness."[82]

There is considerable debate over how to translate what Paul means in Romans 8:26—do we not know "what" or "how" to pray? Either translation is interpretively problematic. In referring to "inarticulate groans,"[83] or "groans that words cannot express,"[84] is Paul attempting to convey what is "unspeakable," that is, impossible, or unpermitted to disclose? Is it an issue of humility or inability? Either way, at least in Corinth, what the enthusiasts there regard as proof of their "arrival" Paul uses as a signal of distance yet to travel.[85] Commenting on prayer in Paul's writings, Dunn says that what is evidenced again and again is "the two sides of charismatic consciousness: the consciousness of human impotence, and the consciousness of divine power in and through weakness."[86] Our groans and stammerings, even our tongues praying, are not signals of our arrival, but rather, represent a calling out for even greater grace and liberty.

[82] Krister Stendhal, "Paul at Prayer," *Meanings: The Bible as Document and as a Guide* (Philedelphia, Fortress Press, 1984) p. 155.
[83] Revised English Bible.
[84] New International Version.
[85] A. J. M. Wedderburn, "Romans 8:26—Towards a Theology of Glossolalia?" *Scottish Journal of Theology*, Vol. 28, 1975, pp. 369–77.
[86] Dunn, p. 242.

* * *

This recognition calls forth a sensitive set of issues with respect to intercessory prayer. It has been a tremendous privilege to work with the members of the ministry team at the Toronto Airport Vineyard and to join with other teams from churches around the world. While these men and women characteristically have hearts as big as all outdoors, it is quickly admitted they do not live out their lives in perfect peace, perfect freedom, or perfect health. This last one is especially problematic. Fee puts the issue squarely:

> How can there be miracles, but no miracle in one's own behalf? How can one glory in the power of the resurrection and the life of the Spirit and not appropriate it for oneself regarding physical weaknesses and sufferings? "Physician heal thyself" was not just a word spoken to Christ; it is always the bottom line of those for whom God's power can be manifest only in visible and extraordinary ways, who never consider that God's greater glory rests on the manifestation of His grace and power through the weakness of the human vessel, precisely so there will never be any confusion as to the Source![87]

As champion of the Spirit, Paul is adamant that while we are "captives in Christ's triumphal procession," we

[87] Fee, p. 824.

are yet the glorious Church triumphant. He quickly moves from recounting the heights of his spiritual ecstasies, and the several revelations he had in the Spirit, to a larger and far more explicit and detailed consideration of his struggle with his "thorn.in the flesh." In this passage in 2 Corinthians 12, as well as in Romans 8, the Apostle is unapologetic: infirmity is not incompatible with, or a contradiction of, life in the Spirit. Rather, in the midst of weakness, broken-ness and failure, even death, the "life of Jesus may be revealed."[88] Paul declares it as bluntly as he can: *We die, and Christ lives in us.*

Paul refuses to conclude that weakness makes him any less spiritual, nor does it diminish the Spirit's work and authority over his life. But neither does he give the last word to suffering. Paul is able to live in the "radical middle" in ways a majority of Christians cannot or will not.[89]

The question, however, still stands: how does one hold signs, and wonders, and a remarkable outpour-ing of God's blessing in tension with seemingly unrelenting suffering and pain? The tendency is to swing to an either–or extreme. There have been movements on both poles—that suffering is to be embraced, for "the flesh must be punished"; alterna-tively, one can name it and claim it, that we have not because we ask not.

[88] 2 Corinthians 4:11.
[89] Fee, p. 825.

It is as though Hebrews 11:32–38 was written with the view to holding forth this very tension: "Some through faith overthrew kingdoms ... and their weakness was turned to strength.... Others were tortured to death, sawn in two, deprived, oppressed, ill-treated." Both the victor and the vanquished are commended and upheld as models of faith and faithfulness. The Spirit's presence and power are demonstrated in both, either through miraculous signs and wonders or by profound joy in the midst of severe hardships.

On both fronts, we "pray in the Spirit." In Ephesians 6:18, this admonition is set in the context of spiritual warfare and spiritual covering. Believers are to find their strength not in their own ability and resource, but "in the Lord, in His mighty power."[90] Recalling Romans 8:26, we do not know how or what to pray; it is for this reason that we need to "pray in the Spirit," so as to know the Lord's strength and imparted resources and thus be able to stand strong against all the forces that seek to overcome us.

The next few verses of the letter to the Ephesians sound the end and purpose of God's call upon our lives: Paul makes it clear that spiritual warfare is *not* that end; rather, it is the call to mission and evangelism. In the Spirit, it is not just that we stand strong against our foe; by the grace of God, we are bold, authorized, and empowered to make Christ known.

[90] Ephesians 6:10.

*   *   *

One night, the Danish philosopher-theologian Søren Kierkegaard had a dream. It serves as conclusion to the considerations of this chapter, for it is a delightful picture of what it means to be in Christ, and to live and pray in the power of the Spirit as resurrection men and women. Kierkegaard wrote of it this way:

> Something wonderful has happened to me. I was caught up into seventh heaven, and I stood in the very presence of God. By special grace, I was granted the privilege of making a wish.
>
> "Will you have youth, or beauty, or power, or the most beautiful of maidens, or any of the other glories there are to be offered? Choose, but only one thing."
>
> For a moment I was at a loss. And then the words came:
>
> "My Lord and my God, I choose this one thing, that I may always have the laugh on my side."
>
> There was silence. Not a word was spoken; I wondered if I had chosen badly.
>
> Then came God's response: *He* laughed.
>
> I realized that my wish had been granted, and then discovered something about God as He laughed—how unsuitable it would have been for Him to answer gravely, "Your wish is granted."[91]

[91] Soren Kierkegaard, *Either/Or*, Vol. I, trans. David Swenson (Princeton, N. J., Princeton University Press, 1959) p. 42. The text has been slightly amended.

CHAPTER FOUR

THIS LOVE IS LIKE A GREAT FIRE

Teresa of Avila and John Calvin on Prayer

With deep roots and firm foundations may you,
in company with all God's people, be strong to
grasp what is the breadth and length and height
and depth of Christ's love, and to know it,
though it is beyond knowledge. (Ephesians
3:18–19)

* * *

In his classic work, *The Varieties of Religious*
Experience, William James draws the conclusion that

our normal waking consciousness, rational consciousness as we call it, is but one special type of
consciousness, whilst all around it, parted from
it by the filmiest of screens, there lie potential
forms of consciousness entirely different....
How to regard them is the question—for they
are so discontinuous with ordinary consciousness. Yet they may determine attitudes though
they cannot furnish formulas, and open a region
though they fail to give a map. At any rate, they

forbid a premature closing of our accounts with reality.[1]

Through their writings and reflections, the Apostles John, Luke, and Paul have enabled us to peek behind the filmy screen, and have demonstrated that in terms of life in the Spirit, far more is at work than many of us have been content to live with. The thing is, not all visions, messages, voices, and knowings are from God. How do we discern what *is* divinely revealed, what is up and out of our own imaginations, and what has a darker source? With all that goes on in meetings that are characterized by the "Toronto Blessing," many feel unsettled by that which is so subjective and experiential. In the Apostle's words, what about "deep roots and firm foundations"?

We do well to glean from the wisdom and understanding of those who have gone before us. To ground our experience in the history of the larger Church serves to anchor what seems to many to be so very new and unprecedented in their own experience. But this requires of us an openness to engage with what might seem unfamiliar territory. For instance, in 1985, I was reading the classics of Christian spirituality for my doctoral residency, and one of the texts I studied was Teresa of Avila's autobiography. Now, ten years later, I have pulled down my copy and reread her

[1] William James, *The Varieties of Religious Experience* (New York, Mentor Books, 1958) p. 298.

Life, with an appreciation I didn't have on the first pass. Much of what I originally concluded to be pretty far-out, misguided, even deluded, I now found insightful and astute; given what the past year had held, and all that we had experienced at the Toronto Airport Vineyard, I read Teresa's observations on life in the Spirit with new understanding. Teresa's writings are called forth in the following pages, not as a validating authority, but as guiding counsel, as we seek to pray in the midst of all that's been experienced through the "Toronto Blessing."

Teresa had to address aspects of her spiritual experience that have striking parallels to those who have found themselves "Toronto Blessed." If we recognize at the outset that Teresa is writing of her personal and typically private encounter with God, her disclosure and reflections act as helpful counsel to what many are experiencing in both corporate worship during public meetings and in their aloneness with God. Several of Teresa's accounts will even serve as a reality check for some; that, because they are having difficulty processing what they're seeing, hearing, and feeling. As I travel around, I'm frequently taken aside towards the end of the meeting and asked what I think about a particular experience of the Spirit. After the teaching that people have just heard me give, they hope I might be of some help. For instance, one gentleman told me that he had seen angels on repeated occasions and wondered if he was losing it. He had tried telling his story to his pastor and several others, and they had left him feeling, as he put it, "a sandwich short of a picnic."

*　*　*

Teresa was a Catholic nun, and from 1531 to 1582 lived in a convent near Madrid, Spain, eventually serving as the Mother Superior to her order. All things considered, she lived a remarkably balanced life of personal devotion and church involvement. The historian Urban Holmes has high praise for her, stating that "there has probably never been a more healthy Christian than Teresa."[2] That's quite a statement, and not without foundation. William James, for instance, features Teresa not in the chapters on "The Sick Soul" or "The Divided Self," but rather in "The Value of Saintliness." That, because in her autobiography, one can trace a deep trust in both people and creation itself; Teresa's was a profound hope in God's sovereign authority over her life and all of history itself. With this faith, she had a sustaining sense of grace and unmerited favour that called forth ongoing gratitude, as well as an openness and courage to meet that which was new and challenging. A reformer in her own right, she brought a lasting leadership to bear on her monastic order, the Carmelites. On a one-to-one basis, she served as a spiritual counsellor to many of her sisters, and through her writings, to thousands and thousands of Christian readers.

[2] Urban Holmes, *A History of Christian Spirituality* (New York, Seabury Press, 1981) p. 99.

Teresa lived during the time of the Inquisition: an extended time of unrest, religiously and politically. Fear was epidemic, intolerance was rife, and even a minor deviation from orthodoxy and the dictates of the Church were suspect to Grand Inquisitors like the infamous Torquemada. In Teresa's day, reports of visions, voices, raptures, and ecstasies were not deemed impossible, but their doctrinal and theological integrity were considered questionable. So, at the request of her superiors, Teresa was required to give an account of her life, for the stories of her spiritual experiences were suspicious.

Though she felt she had no ability and declared that she had no desire to write, she obeyed. Teresa's aim was to describe candidly what she felt and experienced; her attention focussed on the revelations she received from God. In this, she tried to steer through her own personal experiences of the Lord's love for her, what she understood of the Scriptures, and what the Church authorities had taught and expected of her.

One of these expectations was that visions would appear to the physical eye and words would be heard with the actual ear—Teresa's candid declarations established spiritual precedent that such revelations need not necessarily be purely "physical" in nature, but rather, that the "eyes" and "ears" of the spirit can perceive revelations beyond what is disclosed to our senses. Her writings on prayer have been bestsellers for centuries. Teresa's story is of a young, unbalanced, self-willed, and self-centred woman who was transformed by the profound encounters she had with the Spirit of the risen Christ.

Early in her adult life, she had to bear severe physical pain. At one point, an "attack" left her insensible for four days. Teresa thought she was dying; she received the Sacrament of Extreme Unction ("last rites"); her sisters gave her up for dead, and a grave was even left open for her in the convent's cemetery!

She slowly recovered, but for an extended time could not move any of her limbs. Over the next three years she gradually grew stronger, but often could move about only by crawling on her hands and knees. Writing about the experience years later, she prays reflectively:

> O my God, how I longed for the health to serve You better, and this was the cause of all my undoing!... I always thought that I should serve God much better if I recovered. This is our mistake, never to resign ourselves absolutely to what the Lord does, though He knows best what suits us.[3]

Through this season of intense physical suffering, she touched something of the same grace in weakness the Apostle Paul wrote of in 2 Corinthians 12, and with it a deepening of relational intimacy with her Lord. She says: "I believe that my soul gained great strength

[3] *The Life of Saint Teresa*, trans. J. M. Cohen (Edinburgh, Penguin Books, 1957) p. 47.

from His Divine Majesty, and that He must have heard my lamentations and taken pity on all my tears. A desire to spend more time with Him began to grow in me."[4] She often felt, unexpectedly, a strong sense of the presence of God. This was nothing that she could manufacture; she enjoyed her private devotions, but her spiritual disciplines had a disproportionately small part in what she received as "entirely God-given."

Like many who have been "Toronto Blessed," Teresa struggled with the external accusation and the internal fear that she was being deceived, that what she was experiencing was the work of the devil. Again, as she reflects on this time, she has learned that "the One who gives us the blessings will also give us the grace to detect the devil when he begins to tempt us in this way, and make us strong enough to resist him."[5]

* * *

As to *how* we receive God's blessings, Teresa gives extended counsel, found preeminently in her instruction on prayer. The simile she uses for this teaching is a garden in the dry Spanish countryside—a spiritual garden—which produces good fruit to the Lord's pleasure and glory. She uses such a common, familiar illustration because she felt that what she had experienced was nothing special, that every Christian could know and experience the fullest gifts God had for

[4] Cohen, p. 69.
[5] Cohen, p. 72.

them; the only limitation she notes is whether we want that much of God.

As we begin to turn our lives to God in prayer, the gracious Master Gardener, the Lord, begins to root up the weeds in our lives and put in good plants, instead. Teresa says that it's through prayer that we help these tender plants to grow and produce flowers, which with their beauty and bouquet delight our Lord, so much so that we will frequently enjoy His presence as He comes "to take pleasure in this garden...."[6]

She suggests that there are four ways of watering this garden. First, water can be drawn from a well; this is almost too much work. Second, we could use a water wheel and buckets, worked by a windlass. This is easier and brings up more water. Third, water could be channelled across to the garden from a stream or spring. Last, the garden could be watered by heavy rain, when the Lord waters it Himself without any labour of ours.

Teresa then applies these four methods of maintaining the garden to what she understands as four stages of prayer, which she has herself experienced. As an aside, she prays:

> May the Lord graciously grant that I may speak in such a way as to be of use to one of the persons who commanded me to write this, whom the Lord has advanced in four months far beyond the point that I have reached in seventeen years.

[6] Cohen, p. 78.

Without any labour on his part, his garden is watered by all these four means, and, as things are going, with the Lord's help, his garden will soon be submerged. If my way of explaining all this seems crazy to him, he is welcome to laugh at me.[7]

Prayer in the first stage—watering by bucket—is devotional, disciplined prayer. For example, when we think and reflect on the Lord's sufferings in His betrayal and crucifixion for us, it moves us to compassion. To think of the undying love that the Lord has for us and to reflect on His glorious resurrection can stir within us what Teresa calls a "virtuous joy." She says we can picture ourselves as in the presence of Christ, and talk to Him and ask Him for what we need, and "complain to Him of our troubles and rejoice with Him in our pleasures."[8]

She says: "I think that I have made this clear, though perhaps only to myself."[9]

This kind of prayer Teresa considers as prayer of the intellect, where the mind is active and determinative. To the actively cerebral, she suggests a "Sabbath rest." Teresa has been around long enough to know that these types will consider such a spiritual time-out a waste of time, but she says: "I consider this waste a

[7] Cohen, p. 78.
[8] Cohen, p. 84.
[9] Cohen, p. 86.

very great gain. Let them picture themselves, as I have suggested, as in the presence of Christ, and without tiring their minds, let them talk and rejoice with Him."[10] This, because she recognizes that there's a "difference between understanding a thing and knowing it by experience."

This is one of the dynamisms at work in the midst of this current outpouring of God's Spirit, and is succinctly expressed in a thank-you letter I received from Cape Town. An Anglican pastor had been to a Catch the Fire conference at which I was speaking. During ministry time, I had prayed for him, and had prayed something along the lines of "Duncan, preach not *what* you know, but Who you know...." He wrote: "In God's grace, I gave myself to do that tonight. It is now well nigh midnight and I have just returned from our evening service. The Lord really 'showed up' to use Vineyard jargon. People were falling over like nine pins and weeping, laughing and there was all manner of very un-Anglican behaviour! Deep things were happening in many lives that I have been ministering to for a long time. This sort of thing has not happened before. This is amazing...."

* * *

Teresa says that in the second stage, water for the garden is drawn by means of a windlass, and the gardener is able to take some rest instead of being continuously

[10] Cohen, p. 92.

at work. Teresa applies this description to the "prayer of quiet," which she names as that internal "recollection" where we work at silencing our internal noise and begin to attend to the stirrings of the Spirit. Even these beginnings are a given, because they are not something that we, on our own, could possibly attain by our own efforts; rather, it is because it is the Lord's pleasure to reveal Himself to us, in ways such that we realize His nearness. In terms of the garden, Teresa says that by means of the windlass, "the water of great blessing" is more easily accessible because grace is revealed to us with greater power. She says:

> The will alone is occupied in such a way that it is unconsciously taken captive. It simply consents to be God's prisoner, since it well knows how to surrender to One whom it loves. O Jesus, my Lord, how precious Your love is to us then! It binds our own love so closely to it as to leave us no liberty to love anything but You![11]

Though Teresa doesn't use the terms, she recognizes both God's omniscience and omnipresence when she says: "It seems absurd to say this, since we know that God always understands us and is always with us. But our Lord wants us to understand that He understands us, and to realize the effect of His presence." This realization comes as He imparts to our

[11] Cohen, p. 98.

THIS LOVE IS LIKE A GREAT FIRE

hearts a "great inward and outward satisfaction," whereby He seems to be filling up the void that was "scooped out by our sins." Through this gifting, "a little spark of true love" is kindled, and with it we have a greater comprehension of the essence of God's love, and with this revelation an experience of its attendant joy.[12]

*   *   *

The third way of drawing water requires even less effort. All that is necessary is to redirect a stream or creek by means of an irrigation ditch. In terms of prayer and grace that's received, Teresa writes that there comes a blessed confusion; we don't know whether to "speak or be silent; whether to laugh or weep. It is a glorious bewilderment, a heavenly madness, in which true wisdom is acquired, and to the soul a fulfilment most full of delight."[13] In ways that sound very similar to the thousands who have testified over the past year, Teresa says of the sweetness of her experiences that she often found herself "intoxicated with love." She is quick to say that she could not explain or understand "the way in which He worked here."

Teresa candidly admits that the intellect is of no help; what rises up is a longing to pour out one's heart in praise—this experience of God's love is so strong

[12] Cohen, p. 105.
[13] Cohen, p. 112.

that she describes it as "sweet unrest, for it cannot contain itself."[14]

Repeatedly Teresa finds herself at a loss for words to describe this sort of joy. That, for two reasons: one, she finds that it is, in the words of 1 Peter 1:8, "joy inexpressible"; and two, that she is too overcome with it to function:

> Since I write this I am still under the power of that heavenly madness, the effect of Your goodness and mercy. O Lord, I implore You that all those with whom I converse may also become mad through your love. I wish that everyone I meet were afflicted with this same infirmity. I beseech You, Father, let us all be mad, for the love of Him who was called so for Your sake.[15]

As she reflects on her experience, Teresa concludes that the consequence of this loving madness is deep refreshing, for this "water" is life giving, the very nurture that produces rich, ripe fruit. Once experienced, this outpouring of grace stands in striking contrast to drier times; Teresa would presumably have agreed with a term used at Toronto Airport Vineyard, that of "accelerated grace," whereby in this outpouring, the Spirit of God seems to accomplish often in the space of hours of ministry what seemed to have taken years to begin

---

[14] Cohen, p. 113.
[15] Cohen, p. 114.

addressing. Teresa writes: "[W]hat the poor soul has not been able to collect in perhaps twenty years of exhausting effort, the heavenly Gardener gives it in a moment."[16] Again reflecting one of the declarations made repeatedly in our present experience, some of the fruit that grows quickly under these conditions is a profound humility and gratitude. This should come as no surprise, given that one must freely recognize that we do absolutely nothing but accept and receive the Lord's loving graces.

* * *

The fourth means of drawing water involves no labour on our part whatsoever. There is no sense, Teresa says, of anything but enjoyment. The water is now heaven-sent rain, soaking and saturating the whole garden. It is the sort of rain that usually comes when least expected.

The soul is conscious that it is fainting almost completely away in a kind of swoon, with a very great calm and joy. Its breath and all its bodily powers progressively fail it, so that it can hardly stir its hands without the greatest effort. Its eyes close involuntarily, and if they remain open, they see almost nothing.

The ability to speak is gone; physical strength diminishes, while the strength of the spirit increases—and the outward joy that is experienced is "great and most perceptible."

[16] Cohen, p. 117.

However long it may last, it does no harm; at least, it has never done any to me.... Indeed, I am generally much better for it. What harm can possibly be done by so great a blessing? The outward effects are so noteworthy that there can be no doubt some great thing has taken place: we experience a loss of strength but the experience is one of such delight that afterwards our strength grows greater....

The superabundance of the grace granted to the soul clearly indicates how bright has been the sun that has shone upon it and has thus caused the soul to melt away.... With all this happening, the time spent in prayer may last, and does last, for some hours, for, once we have [become] inebriated with the taste of this Divine wine, we are very ready to lose ourselves in order to gain more.[17]

While struggling to put this into words, Teresa was praying after receiving Communion, and the Lord said to her: "I would have you rest more and more in Me. It is no longer you who live; it is I. You cannot comprehend what you understand; you understand by not understanding."

She comments:

[17] *The Life of Teresa of Jesus*, trans. E. Allison Peers (New York, Image Books, Doubleday, 1991) p. 179.

Anyone who has experienced this will to some extent understand. It cannot be expressed more clearly, since all that happens is so obscure. I can only say that the soul conceives itself to be near God, and that it is left with such a conviction that it cannot possibly help believing.... The will is fully occupied in loving, but it does not understand how it loves. If it understands, it does not understand how it understands, or at least, cannot comprehend anything of what it understands. Nor can I myself understand this.[18]

In terms of this not understanding, some would find such surrender objectionable, even scandalous. After all, the Lord has given us in Christ a sound mind. True, but we, especially in the West, are heirs to a hyper-rationalism that is so left brained that we have little honour for anything we can't dissect and reduce to first principles. One of the songs that has been written in the midst of this outpouring is especially provocative at this very point. The first verse of David Ruis's "Sweet Wind" says that we don't know where this wind comes from, and we don't know where it's going, but hey, "let it blow over me." To many of the visitors, it is what's considered typically Vineyard— laid-back, hang-loose, easy-breezy, reckless—and dangerous. "Don't know where it comes from"?—what of its roots? "Don't know where it's going"?—what of its

[18] Peers, p. 127.

fruits? Such uncritical abandon could open us up to
any measure of spirits of deception.

The thing is, David pinched the words for his song
from Jesus, in John 3:8: "The wind blows where it
wills; you do not know where it comes from, or where
it goes."

Teresa reflects on the consequences of this kind of
abandoned encounter with God's Spirit: in it, she
experienced "a very great tenderness, and tears of joy."
That, and a "humility that grows greater." There
comes the recognition that no efforts of our own
could ever help us to gain or keep God's "immeasurable favour."[19] Again, Jesus's conversation with
Nicodemus resounds: "[F]lesh gives birth to flesh; it is
Spirit that gives birth to spirit."

For Teresa, all of this has explicit end: this is not
just personal blessing, but rather, with this growth in
the love of God, there comes an ability, and desire, to
share with others what it has freely received, with the
knowledge that there will be no lack of heavenly treasure. "It prays to God that it may not be rich alone,
and begins to benefit its neighbours, almost uncon-
sciously."[20]

Commenting on the soil on which the rain falls,
Teresa says: "If the ground is well dug over by trials,
persecutions, detractions, and infirmities—few can
reach this point without them—and if it is well broken

[19] Cohen, p. 128.
[20] Cohen, p. 129.

up by extreme detachment from self-interest, it will soak up so much water that it will hardly ever be parched again." But if we should compromise the grace of God with wilful sin, ingratitude, or careless-ness, we may well bring on drought, and our "gar-den" may be given up for lost. However, Teresa is confident that God is ever merciful, and if we will repent, the Lord will again pour out grace upon grace: "for tears gain everything; and one kind of water attracts another."[21]

If not delighted with the rock beat, Teresa would have been of one mind with the lyrics of Ruis's "Sweet Wind," for she is completely trusting of God's faith-fulness: "Come what may, we must risk everything and leave ourselves in God's hands. We have to go willingly wherever we are carried, for in fact, we are being borne off whether we like it or not."[22]

At least as Teresa tells it, these words were no empty rhetoric. She says that she found herself so "carried away" in the Spirit that it affected her whole body, such that it was actually lifted from the ground, and that, on more than one occasion! She says, apologeti-cally: "This has only happened rarely. Once, however, it took place when we were all together in the choir."[23] This levitation distressed and embarrassed her, for "it seemed likely to arouse considerable talk." As she was

[21] Cohen, p. 129.
[22] Cohen, p. 137.
[23] Cohen, p. 137.

prioress, she ordered her nuns not to speak of it. Another time, during preaching, she lay on the ground and had several of her sisters hold her down, unsuccessfully. Such "outward and visible signs" led her to reflect:

> These effects are very striking. One of them is the manifestation of the Lord's mighty power: as we are unable to resist His Majesty's will, either in soul or in body, and are not our own masters, we realize that, however irksome this truth may be, there is One stronger than ourselves, and that these favours are bestowed by Him, and that we, of ourselves, can do absolutely nothing. This imprints in us great humility.[24]

So awesome was this revelation of God's power that, not surprisingly, generated a certain measure of trepidation. But as Teresa lived with the experience awhile, she found that God had met her fears and "overpowered [them] by the deepest love, newly enkindled," so much so that it seemed to her that He seemed not only satisfied with actually raising her spirit to Himself, but that He would have her body, also.[25] Especially with levitation in view, Teresa understates things when she says, "We play no part in bringing a rapture on."

[24] Peers, p. 192.
[25] Cohen, p. 138.

* * *

One of the things that got Teresa into trouble with her superiors was that she heard voices internally. In explaining as exactly as she could what it was she heard, she mapped for others a helpful grid for evaluating what many nowadays understand to be revelatory giftings.

Teresa taught that the words she heard were perfectly formed; she heard them distinctly, but not with her ears. Even so, she maintained that what was spoken was received with greater clarity than if it had been heard audibly. Further, Teresa said that however hard she tried to resist or ignore what was being "spoken," it was impossible to shut it out. She says: "When God speaks to the soul like this, there is no alternative; I have to listen whether I like it or not, and to devote my whole attention to understanding what God wishes me to understand. It makes no difference whether I want to or not."[26]

Though she rarely uses the word, what she describes could be understood in terms of the prophetic: "I have been told things two or three years beforehand that have afterwards been fulfilled, and so far none of them has proved untrue." With great simplicity, she learned to differentiate the revelations of the Spirit from any others: when a word had its source in anything but the Lord, she said that it was like

[26] Cohen, p. 174.

something indistinct, as if she were asleep; "but when God speaks, the voice is so clear that not a syllable of what He says is lost."[27]

In helping those unfamiliar with such revelations, both those who were investigating her theological integrity and her fellow sisters seeking to experience a greater intimacy with God, Teresa lays a rock-solid foundation for the discernment of any given "word": it comes from God only if it conforms to Holy Scripture. "If it diverges in the least from that, I think I should feel incomparably more certain that it came from the devil than I have previously been of its divine origin."[28]

This grounding settled Teresa's fears and uncertainties, which, for an extended time, bothered her considerably. Several of her superiors had been insisting that what she was hearing was of the devil. Understandably, this counsel greatly disturbed her. It was nothing other than a revelation from the Lord that settled the issue for her. She speaks of the experience at some length:

When I was in this terrible state of exhaustion— for at that time I had not yet had a single vision—these words alone were sufficient to remove it and give me complete tranquillity: "Be not afraid, daughter, for it is I and I will not forsake you: fear not."

[27] Cohen, p. 175.
[28] Cohen, p. 175.

In the state I was in at the time, I think it would have needed many hours to persuade me to be calm and no single person would have sufficed to do so. Yet here I was, calmed by nothing but these words and given fortitude and courage, security, tranquillity, and enlightenment, so that in a moment I found my soul transformed.[29]

Probably the greatest single accusation that is brought against the ministry of the Airport Vineyard is that the whole "blessing" is based on deception; that the laughter and the other manifestations, as well as all that is reported to be revelatory, are nothing but the stratagems of the evil one, whose purpose is to deceive even the saints, "if that were possible."[30] One wonders if Teresa was not wearied by similar accusations, for she certainly cuts to the chase when she declares: "I do not understand these fears which make us cry: 'The devil! the devil!', when we might be saying, 'God! God!', and making the devil tremble."[31]

*   *   *

Teresa was no stranger to physical manifestations as she experienced the power of God's love. Often she simply called these "impulses." Sometimes the manifestations

[29] Ward, p. 241.
[30] Matthew 24:24. It should be noted that this verse in context warns against those claiming to be Messiah and prophets. It is not an indictment of "signs and wonders." These are presumed.
[31] Cohen, p. 183.

were so strong that she could not physically move. She notes more than once that her "natural strength failed."[32] Early on, this was a cause for embarrassment; she records the way the Lord led her through this time:

> Once when I was extremely worried about this, the Lord asked me what I was afraid of, for only one of two things could happen: either they would speak ill of me or praise Him. By this He meant that those who believed it was His work would praise Him, and those who did not would condemn me.[33]

As Marc Dupont at the Airport Vineyard has noted, one of the definitions for the word *dignity* is "self-possession"; many of the manifestations leave us in quite undignified positions and states. Once we've concluded that God's love is at source, then with Teresa, we can find freedom in the truth that one of two things will happen: people will speak ill of us for our behaviour, or praise God for the wonderful work He's accomplishing within us as we abandon ourselves to His grace.

Teresa was repeatedly overcome with a glorious joy: "I was so bewildered and foolish that I did not know what to do, or how I could have received this great favour and grace. Such was my inward rejoicing that,

[32] Cohen, p. 286.
[33] Cohen, p. 226.

as you might say, I could neither hear nor see."[34]
Another time she stated: "This revelation is accompanied by a joy so sublime as to be indescribable. All the
senses are filled with such a profound bliss and sweetness that no description is possible. It is better, therefore, to say no more about this."[35] Like the majority of
those testifying to their experience of "blessing,"
Teresa says that with this gift of joy came a release
from her fears, and in their place "a great tranquillity
and inward delight." As though giving personal testimony, and mirroring interviews conducted at meetings currently held, Teresa reflects: "Often a person
who was previously very ill, and racked with severe
pain, is left healthy at the end and stronger than
before. For a very great gift is received in rapture, and
the Lord sometimes wishes the body, as I have said, to
enjoy it also, because at such times it is obedient to
the will of the soul."[36] Reflecting on this transformation, she says: "And what are these joys that the Lord
gives us? Only one drop of water from the great, overflowing river that He has prepared for us."[37]

As she found herself deeper and deeper in this river,
Teresa struggled to express the revelations she
received: "When the Lord is pleased to reveal so much
of His greatness and majesty to it, the vision has such
great strength that I think it would be impossible to

[34] Cohen, p. 287.
[35] Cohen, p. 284.
[36] Cohen, p. 138.
[37] Cohen, p. 192.

bear it, unless the Lord were pleased to help the soul in a most supernatural way." Regarding her overall state, she says simply: "It is always intoxicated."

As the Lord made Himself known to Teresa, she was further and further filled with awe:

> It is like a man who has had no schooling, and has never even taken the trouble to learn to read, yet who finds himself, without any study, in possession of all living knowledge. He does not know how or whence it came, since he has never done even so much work as would be necessary for learning the alphabet.... For the soul suddenly finds itself learned, and such exalted mysteries as that of the Holy Trinity are so plain to it that it would boldly argue against any theologian in defence of these miraculous truths.[38]

Teresa is adamant that such revelations are pure grace, and are absolutely unearned and undeserved: "Reflect on this truth: that God gives Himself to those who give up everything for Him. He is no respecter of persons, but loves everyone, with no exceptions, as He was pleased, in His goodness, that I should see."[39]

Similar declarations of gratitude recur throughout her autobiography. She says again and again that there is *nothing* we can do to bring things on:

[38] Cohen, p. 192.
[39] Cohen, p. 192.

No effort of ours makes us see more or less, or calls up or dispels a vision. The Lord desires us to see very clearly that this work is not ours but His Majesty's. We are the less able, therefore, to take pride in it; on the contrary it makes us humble and afraid, when we see that just as the Lord takes away our power of seeing what we will, so He can also remove these favours and His grace, with the result that we are utterly lost.[40]

*　*　*

There are, throughout the accounts of religious experience, records of angelic visitation. This is certainly the case with the Scriptures: Abraham, Jacob, Moses, Balaam, Elijah, David, Daniel, Joseph, Mary, Elizabeth and Zachariah, the shepherds, and the Apostles Peter, Philip, Paul, and John are all the subjects of angelic revelations. The history of the Church adds its complement, and Teresa is one of this company. Her accounts may serve those who are the subjects of this present day:

Beside me, on the left hand, appeared an angel in bodily form, such as I am not in the habit of seeing except very rarely. Though I often have visions of angels, I do not see them.... He was not tall but short, and very beautiful; and his face was so aflame that he appeared to be one of the

[40] Cohen, p. 206.

highest rank of angels, who seem to be all on fire.... In his hands I saw a great golden spear, and at the iron tip there appeared to be a point of fire. This he plunged into my heart several times so that it penetrated to my entrails. When he pulled it out, I felt that he took them with it, and left me utterly consumed by the great love of God. The pain was so severe that it made me utter several moans.

Understating the experience, she says: "Throughout the days that this lasted I went about in a kind of stupor."[41] This was not a singular revelation. Teresa describes another of the visions whereby the door into the heavens was thrown wide open, and she says she beheld the throne of God, around which was a great multitude of angels, "seemingly all on fire," the glory that, she says, "cannot be expressed in writing."[42] The experience left her in a "state of bliss" for two hours.

Recently, Dr. David Hope, the bishop of London, commented on some of the phenomena witnessed in churches experiencing the "Toronto Blessing." He said, "I don't mind them falling down. What I want to know is whether they are any good when they get up!" Teresa writes at length about what was the focus

[41] Cohen, p. 210.
[42] Cohen, p. 303.

or the purposed end of all the manifestations and revelations:

> There grew so great a love of God within me that I did not know who had planted it there. It was entirely supernatural; I had made no efforts to obtain it.... He is increasing my desire to serve Him, and quickening my love for Him.... The Lord often says to me, as a sign of His great love: "Now you are Mine and I am yours" ... "Ah, daughter," He said to me, "how few there are that truly love Me, for if they did so I would not hide My secrets from them! Do you know what it is to love Me truly? It is to know that everything which is not pleasing to Me is a lie."[43]

Injected into her reflections on her experiences are bursts of praise: "O God, may You be blessed for ever, for now I see that You loved me far more than I love myself."[44]

* * *

Hearing voices and seeing visions have often been regarded as hysterical phenomena. In her own day, the overseers of the Inquisition considered Teresa's intimacy with God and her visions, voices, raptures, and ecstasies dubious, not because they thought them

[43] Cohen, pp. 297, 303, 306.
[44] Cohen, p. 235.

impossible, but because they questioned their doctrinal and theological integrity. Like many of the concerns raised about the "Toronto Blessing," this position speaks more of the critics' theological biases and experience than anything else, given that the incarnational birth of Christ, for instance, is announced with visions and angelic encounter, as is the Lord's resurrection. The same revelations are fundamental to Saul's conversion and Peter's understanding of the inclusion of the Gentiles in the outpouring of God's grace. These are the high points in the early life of the Church; even so, the study of Paul's understanding of prayer and the Spirit has demonstrated that the first generation of believers were highly charismatic in the living out of their faith, and that visions, prophecy, ecstatic speech, and worship were both central and dynamic in their personal and corporate lives.

Regardless of what one makes of either Teresa's spiritual experience or her reflections and considerations, few of us should be unchallenged by her trustful humility. Teresa cites Augustine's simple prayer of abandon—"Give me what You ordain, and ordain what You will."[45] Teresa stands in company with those who come forward for prayer at the Toronto Airport Vineyard, not seeking any particular

[45] Augustine, *Confessions*, Book X, Ch. 29. Nicene and Post-Nicene Fathers, First Series, Vol. 1 (Peabody, Mass., Hendrickson Pub., 1994) p. 153b.

manifestation or experience but trusting God's perfect love and His gracious purpose to bless, simply saying, "Whatever, Lord."

With much that is beyond understanding, and for many far outside the range of past experience, Teresa's counsel gives firm grounding to the *more* that is currently being touched: "When it is the Lord's pleasure, there is no measure in His giving.... Let it trust the Giver, and it will learn why He reveals His gifts."[46]

Once, or if, this is recognized, there comes a glorious freedom. In the sovereign authority of God, we don't have to have all the answers, nor do we have to solve all the problems. This is not licence for abdication or irresponsibility, but rather, life and love in Gospel grace that calls forth "all our heart, all our soul, with all our mind, and all our strength."[47] With profound gratitude we live out the ongoing transformation of our lives, knowing that "this love is like a great fire, which has to be fed so that it shall not go out. Whatever it may cost us, we must bring wood to keep the fire alive."[48]

* * *

John Calvin, a contemporary of Teresa's, is an invaluable asset in complementing her reflections on the presence and power of God. His hard-core theology of prayer can be considered fuel for the fire Teresa

[46] Cohen, pp. 277 and 228.
[47] Mark 12:30.
[48] Cohen, p. 221.

named. To change metaphors, Calvin's instruction serves as an anchor pin in the stormy waters of what is by nature highly experiential and subjective. Though Calvin would be unfamiliar and presumably unsettled by the physical manifestations of many who find themselves "Toronto Blessed," there's no way of telling what kind of reflections he would have generated if *his* wife had been "leaping about with transports of joy," or had her "bodily strength overcome." When one has a credible witness, all manner of unusual behaviour requires consideration, processing, and evaluation.

For instance, in 1738 when Jonathan Edwards wrote his commentary on 1 Corinthians 13, entitled *Charity and Its Fruits*, he took the Calvinistic line when it came to verse 8: "Charity never faileth: but whether there be prophecies, they shall fail; whether there be tongues, they shall cease; whether there be knowledge, it shall vanish away."[49] In terms of the prophetic and miraculous graces of God, he comments: "All these were extraordinary gifts bestowed for a season for the introduction and establishment of Christianity in the world, and when this their end was gained, they were all to fail and cease. But charity was never to cease."[50] With the completion and closing of the canon of Scripture, he states: "[T]he miraculous

---

[49] Jonathan Edwards,*Charity and Its Fruits* (Edinburgh, Banner of Truth Trust, 1991) p. 304.
[50] Edwards, p. 306.

gifts of the Spirit were no longer needed.... God caused them to fail because there was no further occasion for them.... We have no reason to expect them any more.... When the apostles and others of their day died and went to heaven, they left all their miraculous gifts behind them with their bodies."[51] Four years later, when he wrote *Thoughts Concerning the Present Revival in New England, the Ways in Which it is to be Acknowledged and Promoted*, he still maintains a cessationist's critique of the abuses of so-called prophetic excesses of the day. Nevertheless, he is completely unapologetic and unashamed of the dynamisms and ecstasies his wife, Sarah, experienced in the power and presence of the Spirit.[52] Without a deep humility, theological prejudices die hard.

* * *

Let's recognize at the outset that there are not many who lovingly embrace the name John Calvin. If the man is known at all, it is the caricature of someone who was against all things soft and beautiful. His Rotterdam portrait depicts a person who is austere, harsh, and intense. Those who have studied some of Calvin's theology may think of words and phrases such as "total depravity," "double predestination," "the Protestant work ethic" or of his life's work, *The Institutes of the*

---

[51] Edwards, pp. 313 and 314.
[52] See *Catch the Fire*, pp. 75–86, or *The Works of Jonathan Edwards*, Vol. 1 (Edinburgh, Banner of Truth Trust, 1992) pp. lxii–lxx and 356–380.

Christian Religion (recalled with a weak and weary heart). More positively, some name themes such as "the sovereignty of God," "providence," a return to "Scriptural Christianity," and a "zeal for godliness," maintaining that these are characteristically Calvin.

If the truth be told, the prejudice against Calvin is based more on the austerities of later Calvin*ism* than on the man himself; when his writings are studied, especially his Bible commentaries and sermons, what emerges is the reformer's passion for God, for Christ's Church, and for the Spirit's inspiration of the Word of God that turns lives around and brings freedom and wholeness. As such, Calvin's understanding and interpretation of the Scriptures continue to serve us as we seek to live out our lives as a worshipping community, attending to the life in Christ to which we are called. This is especially the case given the extent of Calvin's writing on prayer and the place he gives it. In *The Institutes of the Christian Religion*, the longest section of all is devoted to prayer, and serves as a conclusion to his entire theology. He titles his chapter on prayer "The Chief Exercise of Faith, and by Which We Daily Receive God's Benefits."

* * *

Calvin was born in 1509, and during the fifty-five years of his life, he was uncommunicative about his personal history and experience. He wrote no autobiography, and unlike one of his faith heroes, Augustine, he authored nothing like the *Confessions;* he kept no journal. There was in Calvin a certain timidity, an aristocratic inclination to guard himself from public life. There is, therefore, little personal reflection recorded on the inner workings of the Spirit in his life. Rather, Calvin is a systematic writer, and this fact works against an intimate understanding of the man himself. From his letters, tracts and other writings, the outline and essentials of his life can be gleaned, but little else. For instance, Calvin opens the window of his soul but a crack when he writes on the death of his infant son in 1542: "The Lord has certainly inflicted a severe and bitter wound.... But He is himself a Father, and knows what is good for His children."[53] With that, the window is closed.

While there is little that we learn of the intimate workings of the Spirit in Calvin's own prayer life, his general instruction speaks volumes, for he was the first in almost a thousand years to write a detailed and extended exposition of prayer that was essentially grounded in the Scriptures and intended for the laity. In terms of the broad sweep of instruction on the subject of prayer before him, Calvin's "Chief Exercise of Faith" stands in marked contrast to the balance of works produced throughout the Middle Ages, for they were, characteristically, mystical by approach and intended for the monastic community.

In contrast, Calvin's purpose in writing on prayer was to give practical instruction to his fellow believers.

[53] *A Calvin Reader*, ed. William Keesecker (Philadelphia, Westminster Press, 1985) p. 16.

While he writes as a cleric, he addresses the pastoral concerns and needs of his parishioners; his instruction is not for "professionally religious types," but for the reformed laity of middle Europe. In this, Calvin intentionally addresses concerns not dissimilar to those that have generated *Pray with Fire*, namely: how to help a believer pray in the midst of reformation and renewal. Where Teresa is an important resource as she reflects on her *experience* of the Spirit, Calvin serves in laying bare rock-solid foundations for faith and prayer that are laid firmly on the Scriptures.

* * *

For Calvin, the written Word of God is absolutely and incontestably this bedrock. To shift the focus to anything else is to compromise and distract. He uses several metaphors to stress this essential and inseparable relationship:

> There is a permanent relationship between faith and the Word. [The Apostle] could not separate one from the other any more than we could separate the rays from the sun from which they come.... Faith needs the Word as much as fruit needs the living root of a tree (III.2.6 and 31, pp. 548 and 576).[54]

[54] Citations are from Ford Lewis Battles's translation of *The Institutes of Christian Religion* (Philadelphia, Westminster Press, 1960). The numbers in parentheses correspond to the number of the book, the chapter, and the section.

For Calvin, faith joins prayer and the Word. The three are an indispensable unit, three strands of a strong rope. The Word contains the gracious promises of God; moved by the Holy Spirit, the initiator of faith, the believer is enabled to respond to the promises disclosed in the Word; faith is thereby created. But it is only in prayer that this faith becomes active and vital, for in prayer, we "take hold" of all that God promises in Christ. For this reason, Calvin prays:

> Grant, Almighty God, that since we cannot really profit by thy Word in any other way than by having all our thoughts and affections subject to thee and offered to thee as a sacrifice—God, grant that we may suffer thee, by the sound of thy Word, so to pierce through everything within us that, being dead in ourselves, we may live unto thee.[55]

Further, he puts the issue bluntly in his tenth sermon on Psalm 119, maintaining that there is no access for any prayers that are not founded upon the Word.[56] Calvin is insistent that the believer's prayers are to be formed only in the clear light of the Word of God, in accordance with what the Lord has commanded. One does not err when one "reposes on the

---

[55] Micah 2:11, *Comm.*, p. 209.
[56] John Calvin, *Two and Twenty Sermons* (London, John Harifon, 1580) p. 86.

Word and promise of God,"[57] for it is the "sole end and legitimate use of prayer, that we may reap the fruits of God's promises."[58]

This inseparable bond between the Word of God and Christian prayer is one of Calvin's contributions to the history of instruction on private prayer. Given its simplest expression, Calvin would say that our prayers echo God's promises, as they are recorded in the Scriptures, and become for us the *living* Word of God by the power of the Spirit. Repeatedly Calvin teaches a progression from God's promises, to faith, to prayer, to the actualization and realization of those promises.

* * *

Square one for Calvin's overall theology is the "right knowledge of God."[59] It is also the starting point for his instruction on prayer. As to this knowledge, in a sermon entitled "The Privilege of Prayer," Calvin declares:

> This is the true fruit of faith, to know that God is our Father, and to be moved by His love. The way is open for us to run to Him, and it is easy to pray to Him when we are convinced that His eyes are upon us, and that He is ready to help us in all our necessities. [60]

[57] Psalm 7:6, *Comm.*, I p. 81.
[58] Psalm 119:38, *Comm.*, IV p. 428.
[59] *Institutes*, I.1.1.
[60] "Privilege," p. 183.

What we know of God, both intellectually and experientially, is ultimately revealed in Jesus. This knowledge, insists Calvin, is grace, and not something we ever can accomplish on our own: "We are near Him, not as having anticipated His grace, and come to Him of ourselves, but because, in His condescension, He has stretched out His hand as far as hell itself to reach us."[61] Commenting on John 17:20, and Jesus's intercessions, "I pray for those who believe ..." Calvin states:

> This is assuredly a remarkable ground of confidence.... This prayer of Christ's is a safe harbour, and whoever retreats into it is safe from all danger of shipwreck; for it is as if Christ had solemnly sworn that He will devote all care and diligence to our salvation.[62]

As was noted earlier, we have been singing many of our prayers, and Vineyard songwriters, such as Brian Doerksen and Cindy Rethmeier have, as it were, put Calvin's instruction to music:

> I want to know You, Lord I must know You
> I want to be found in You
> I want to be clothed in Your truth
> So I fix my eyes on You, Lord I must see You
> I put my faith in You,

---

[61] Psalm 65, *Comm.*, II p. 457.
[62] John 17:20, *Comm.*, p. 181.

I spend my life on You
I want to know You, I want to love You
I want to know You more ...
Jesus, Jesus, Jesus, Jesus.[63]

* * *

In the introduction to Calvin's instruction on prayer as it is found in the *Institutes,* the good news of Jesus Christ is freely declared as the basis for our prayers:

In Christ [God] offers all happiness in place of our misery, all wealth in place of our neediness; in Him He opens to us the heavenly treasures that our whole faith may contemplate His beloved Son, our whole expectation depend upon Him, and our whole hope cleave to and rest in Him. After we have been instructed by faith to recognize that whatever we need and whatever we lack is in God, and in our Lord Jesus Christ, it remains for us to seek in Him, and in prayers to ask of Him, what we have learned to be in Him. Otherwise, to know God as the master and bestower of all good things, who invites us to request them of Him, and still not go to Him and not ask of Him—this would be of as little profit as for a man to neglect a treasure,

---

[63] "I Want to Know You," Brian Doerksen and Cindy Rethmeier, Mercy Music. Used by permission.

buried and hidden in the earth, after it had been pointed out to him (III.20.1, p. 850).

This is the bedrock on which Calvin erects his teaching on prayer. He states categorically: "We frame our prayers without hesitation or trepidation [when] relying on the word of Him whose majesty would otherwise terrify us, we dare call upon him as Father." (III.20.19, p. 868).

That we might be convinced of this open way to God, Calvin cites lists of Scripture passages that preeminently declare "how gently God attracts us to Himself" (III.20.14, p. 868). The following texts are to ever "resound in our ears" if we are to appropriate the promises of Scripture: Psalm 50:15, "If you call upon Me in time of trouble, I will come to your rescue, and you shall honour Me"; Isaiah 65:24, "Before they call to Me, I will answer, and while they are still speaking I will listen"; Jeremiah 29:12, "If you invoke Me and pray to Me, I will listen to you: when you seek Me, you shall find Me ..."; Romans 10:13, "Everyone who invokes the name of the Lord will be saved"; 1 Peter 5:7, "Cast all your cares on Him, for you are His charge."[64] Salted through his comments on these and similar passages are phrases such as "Who will open his mouth unless assured of God's

---

[64] Cf. Ps. 65:1, 91:15; Ps. 145:18; Is. 30:15; Joel 2:32; Jn. 15:24: Calvin repeatedly excuses his partial inventory stating that "it is not my purpose to list every passage." III.20.14, p. 868.

Fatherly favour?"[65] "Unless persuaded that God takes special notice of each affliction which we endure, it is impossible ... to pray [with] confidence.";[66] "[We] are invited to Him with such gentleness as that nothing may hinder [us] from familiarly and confidently approaching Him."[67] "What is taught here is that [God] bears the character of the best of fathers, who takes pleasure in tenderly cherishing His children, and in bountifully nourishing them."[68] "As faith breaks out into prayer [it] penetrates into the treasures of the grace of God."[69] "God is ever ready to add new blessings to former ones, without any end or limitation ... hence prayer is connected with confidence and certainty as to God's love towards us."[70] With this understanding in hand, it was with far greater hope, awe, confidence, assurance, and freedom that we pray the simple prayer "More, Lord."

* * *

We are not on our own when it comes to actual praying. Early in his teaching from the *Institutes,* Calvin names the Spirit as the "remedy" to help us in our natural inability to live out the life of faith. He is given as our teacher in prayer, "to tell us what is right and temper

[65] Psalm 51:1, *Comm.*, II p. 295.
[66] Psalm 56:8, *Comm.*, II p. 355.
[67] Psalm 102:2, *Comm.*, IV p. 98.
[68] Psalm 104:32, *Comm.*, IV p. 17.
[69] *Harm.*, Mark 11:24, III p. 20.
[70] James 1:6, *Comm.*, p. 283.

our emotions" (III.20.5, p. 855). Further, in his *Commentary* on Romans 8:16, Calvin adds that the Spirit witnesses to our spirits, assuring us of our adoption and giving us the confidence to call upon God as Father. "Except the Spirit testifies to our heart respecting the paternal love of God, our tongues would be dumb, so that they could utter no prayers."[71]

As to the Spirit coming to the aid of our weakness (Romans 8:26), the verb *sunantilambanetai* is understood metaphorically as the help given to infants who are not able to support themselves. This is the very help the Spirit affords, "for as experience shows, except we are supported by God's hands, we are soon overwhelmed by innumerable evils."[72]

In commenting on Romans 8:26 and the Spirit's intercession, Calvin understands this to mean that the Spirit suggests the "manner of praying aright; ... no one can of himself premeditate even one syllable, except God by the secret impulse of his Spirit knocks at our door, and thus opens for Himself our hearts."

Summary instruction on the Spirit's work in the prayer of faith is found in Calvin's comments on Jude 20, "praying in the Spirit." There he says:

No one can pray aright except he be roused by the Spirit of God; ... no one dares to call God his Father, except through the teaching of the same

---

[71] *Comm. on Romans*, p. 299.
[72] Romans 8:26, *Comm.*, p. 311.

Spirit; for from Him is all solicitude, from Him is ardour and vehemence, from Him is alacrity, from Him is confidence in obtaining what we ask.... It is not, then, without reason that Jude teaches us, that no one can pray as he ought without having the Spirit as his guide.[73]

* * *

With this foundational work laid firm, some of Calvin's further reflections serve as we find ourselves "praying in the midst." Calvin makes it clear that there are limits, "fences." It is not anything goes when we come before God in prayer. In the *Genevan Catechism of 1541*, a basic question is asked of prayer: "Can we ask for all that comes into our mind, or is there a certain rule to be observed?" While the question anticipates Calvin's teaching on the Lord's Prayer, the answer nevertheless lays general foundation for framing prayers faithfully:

If we followed our own fantasy, our prayers would be very badly ordered. We are so ignorant that we cannot judge what is good to ask: moreover, all our desires are so intemperate that it is necessary that we should not give them a loose rein.[74]

Similarly, in the *Institutes,* Calvin clearly addresses

[73] *Comm.*, p. 447.
[74] *Cat.*, QA 253, p. 44.

"undisciplined and irreverent prayer," in section 5. After speaking of distractions in prayer, he makes note of the limits placed on the prayers of faith, for while Scripture bids us to pour out our hearts before the Lord (Psalm 62:8) and to cast all our cares on the Lord (I Peter 5:7), God does not "indiscriminately slacken the reins to stupid and wicked emotions" (III.20.5, p. 855).

In the *Commentaries,* Calvin teaches explicitly that prayer must be in conformity with God's will and God's Word. Most simply stated, Calvin holds as an axiom that "our prayers are faulty, so far as they are not founded on the Word."[75] Citing 1 John 5:14 ("if we make requests which accord with His will He will listen to us ..."), Calvin insists that the rule for prayer must be conformity to the divine will. Commenting on Psalm 7:6, he says further:

> We can never pray in faith unless we attend, in the first place, to what God commands, that our minds may not rashly and at random start aside in deserving more than we are permitted to desire and pray for.[76]

In this, prayer is not so much a natural work that we conduct on our own, the conforming of our lives to the things defined in the word of God; rather, it is a

[75] Genesis 19:18, *Comm.,* I p. 509.
[76] *Comm.,* I. 81.

supernatural response that is called forth as we attend to the "inward motions of [God's] Spirit." Calvin lets this spill over a bit, stating:

> Indeed there are three ways in which God acts the part of our teacher, instructing us by His Word, enlightening our minds by the Spirit, and engraving instruction upon our hearts.[77]

Again, we're not left on our own. For instance, in the *Institutes* Calvin writes: "As by the Holy Spirit we understand the Scriptures, so here by the prompting of the Spirit we are guided in prayer" (III.20.6, p. 856). Commenting on Mark 11:20f., he says that the Spirit must hold all our affections "by the bridle of the Word of God, and bring them into obedience."[78] Further, when we pray "in Jesus' name," we limit our wishes to the rule of right praying, for to pray in the name is to desire "the vital sap of the Holy Spirit, which enables one to bear fruit."[79] Commenting on Romans 8:26 and 27 and the pleading of the Spirit within those who pray, Calvin understands this to mean that the Spirit is the director of our prayers, and in this, He conforms our wills to His. Therefore, what is to hold "first place in our prayers is consent with the will of the Lord."[80]

[77] *Comm.*, V p. 256.
[78] *Harm.*, III p. 20.
[79] John 15:7, *Comm.*, p. 111.
[80] *Comm.*, p. 314.

It is in this spirit that the Airport ministry team encourages people to assume the "Whatever, Lord" posture when they come forward for prayer.

Repeatedly Calvin instructs his readers to "cast all their cares into God's kindly bosom."[81] This "unsuspecting confidence" in God's fatherly kindness is the "reverse of those perplexing anxieties which men brood over inwardly to their own distress, and by which they torture themselves, and are chafed by their afflictions rather than be led to God."[82] Calvin calls this "disburdening." In his comments on Jeremiah 33:1-6, "Cry unto me and I will answer," Calvin admonishes: "Whenever we pine away in sorrow, or are worn out by affliction, it is our own fault, because we are tardy and slow to pray."[83] This is because we "disburden our anxieties, as it were, into God's bosom, ... and repose in the providence of God."[84] In his *Commentary* on 1 Peter, he makes his point even more strongly, stating: "We are more than insane, if we knowingly and willfully close up the way to God's presence by prayer, since this is the only asylum of our salvation."[85]

No stranger to tough, even desperate times, Calvin writes at length on the dynamics that sustain perseverance, namely, hope and patience. He lists several

---

[81] Genesis 32:9, *Comm.*, II p. 190; Psalm 37:5, *Comm.*, II p. 21; 1 Thessalonians 5:17, *Comm.*, p. 296; 1 Peter 5:7, *Comm.*, p. 149.
[82] Psalm 142:2, *Comm.*, V p. 245.
[83] *Comm.*, IV pp. 230-31.
[84] I Thessalonians 5:17, *Comm.* p. 296.
[85] *Comm.* p. 100.

Scripture witnesses who vowed to wait on the Lord a favourite being the prophet Habakkuk: "I will stand upon my watch, and set me upon the tower, and will watch to see what He will say unto me."[86] Calvin comments:

> The only means by which, in our affliction, we can obtain the victory, is by our having hope shining in us in the midst of darkness, and by our having the sustaining influence which arises from waiting for the favour of God.[87]

In commenting on Philippians 4:7, he speaks further of the peace of mind and heart that comes as the fruit of hope: "It does not depend on the present aspect of things, and does not bend itself to the various shiftings of the world, but is founded on the firm and immutable Word of God." Further, this peace passes all understanding because

> Nothing is more foreign to the human mind, than in the depth of despair to exercise, nevertheless, a feeling of hope, in the depth of poverty to see opulence, and in the depth of weakness to keep from giving way, and, in fine, to promise ourselves that nothing will be wanting to us when we are left destitute of all things and all this

[86] Habakkuk 2:1.
[87] Psalm 69:13, *Comm.*, III p. 60.

in the grace of God alone, which is not itself known otherwise than through the Word, and the inward earnest of the Spirit.[88]

Elsewhere, Calvin counsels simply to "repose on the Providence of God."[89]

* * *

Throughout *The Institutes of the Christian Religion*, Calvin broadly shapes his writing with two foci in view: the first, the knowledge of God; the second, the knowledge of self (I.1.1, p. 35). This same general treatment is followed in his instruction on prayer. The teaching considered thus far can be understood as grounded in the knowledge of God's Fatherly love and providential care. If the focus is changed from God to the one praying, a whole new set of "rules" must be issued, confession being the first and foremost. So, in section seven, Calvin forthrightly states: "Lawful prayer demands repentance" (III.20.7, p. 858). Section nine of Calvin's chapter on prayer makes this explicit, for there he states:

> To sum up: the beginning, and even the preparation, or proper prayer is the plea for pardon with a humble and sincere confession of guilt ... [for God cannot] be propitious to any but those whom He has pardoned. Accordingly ... believers

[88] *Comm.*, p. 120.
[89] Genesis 24:14, *Comm.*, II p. 18.

open for themselves the door to prayer with this key (III.20.9, p. 860).

This teaching is certainly not confined to the *Institutes*. The Psalms contain many prayers of confession, giving Calvin frequent opportunity to clarify his teaching. Sometimes he simply states: "Whoever would reap profit from the exercise of prayer, must necessarily begin with free remission of sins."[90] Other times, he presses similitude into service to make his point, as in his comments on Psalm 25:7, "Remember not the sins of my youth":

> Our sins are like a wall between us and God, and prevent him from hearing our prayers and stretching forth His hand to help.... Men pray in wrong ways and in vain unless they begin by seeking forgiveness of their sins. The right and proper order of prayer is to ask, at the very onset, that God would pardon our sins.[91]

Not surprisingly, similar teaching is found in Calvin's comments on Luke 18:9, the parable of the Pharisee and the publican. Giving definition to "acceptable prayer," Calvin states that humility is the requisite for coming into the presence of God. He cautions that no disease is more dangerous than arrogance. At the Toronto Airport

---

[90] Psalm 130:4, *Comm.*, V p. 131.
[91] *Comm.*, I p. 419.

THIS LOVE IS LIKE A GREAT FIRE

Vineyard, this is frequently named, and held as an absolute prerequisite for knowing the blessing of God. While it may not be declared in every single sermon or teaching time, it's a rare meeting where it does not feature in at least one of the movements in the worship: at the very least, we have *sung* our confessions, such that many have found themselves weeping, kneeling, even prostrated, as they seek forgiveness for their sin, often at a depth rarely touched before, as the Spirit of God reveals root issues of idolatry, fear, mistrust, and control.

* * *

In the *Genevan Catechism,* Calvin addresses similar concerns in answering "the way of prayer to God." He calls for both understanding and affection, stating: "Since God is Spirit, He always requires the heart, and especially in prayer, in which we enter into communication with Him, wherefore He promises to be near to those only who call upon Him in truth" (Psalm 145:18).[92]

Like Teresa, Calvin's understanding of a life of prayer is characterized by gratitude, for as he states in his *Commentary* on Psalm 50:14–15, 23, it is the "foundation of all prayer, ... the most elementary exercise of faith."[93] He maintains that the heartfelt celebration of God's goodness is the "chief exercise in godliness," and as such, prayers of adoration and praise are to be engaged during the whole of life. This,

[92] *Cat.,* A241, p. 42.
[93] *Comm.,* II p. 270.

because the giving of thanks is the true and proper worship of God, for it is crediting to His generosity and providential caregiving every good that comes to us. Similar sentiment is expressed in the *Institutes*, though with greater passion:

> God does not cease to heap benefits upon benefits in order to impel us, though slow and lazy, to gratefulness. In short, we are well-nigh overwhelmed by so great and so plenteous an outpouring of benefactions, by so many and mighty miracles discerned wherever one looks, that we never lack reason and occasion for praise and thanksgiving.[94]

Further, thanksgiving and petition are held together as the two poles of prayer, the one asking God for help, the other praising Him for His gracious intervention. So, Calvin says, the right form of prayer joins these two affections together, "by reason of the hope which, showing us the haven nigh at hand, doth refresh us even in the midst of shipwreck."[95]

This confidence finds foundation in such biblical assertions as Ephesians 3:20, "Now to him who is able to do exceeding abundantly above all we ask or think ...," leading Calvin to comment: "Whatever expectations we form of Divine blessings, the infinite

[94] *Institutes*, III.20:28, pp. 888–89.
[95] Acts 16:23, *Comm.*, p. 117.

goodness of God will exceed all our wishes and all our thoughts."[96]

Such instruction affords us firm grounding from which to discern and evaluate the testimonies in the chapter that follows.

---

[96] *Comm.*, p. 266.

CHAPTER FIVE

SEVEN OPEN WINDOWS

Testimonies

If your Presence does not go with us, do not send us up from here. How will anyone know that You are pleased with me and with Your people unless You go with us? What else will distinguish me and Your people from all the other people on the face of the earth? (Exodus 33:15–16 NIV)

*   *   *

Along lines similar to the accusations brought against the Great Awakening, reports of the 1904 Welsh revival were greeted by many who felt that it was "much ado about nothing," the mere outworkings of an unbridled emotionalism. A Congregational minister, the Reverend Peter Price, may be considered the leading spokesman against the work; like Charles Chauncy before him, he referred to the revival as the product of fleshly rather than heavenly fire, and that the visitors who came from abroad were seeing nothing but a "shallow, noisy, exhibitionist revival."[1] The

---

[1] Brynmor Jones, *Voices from the Welsh Revival, 1904–1905.* (Worcester, Evangelical Press of Wales, 1995) p. 270.

meetings, some of which went till three and four in the morning, were certainly provocative by some accounts: "Order gave place to confusion. Some were shouting, 'No more, Lord Jesus, or I die!' The noise of weeping, singing and praising, together with the sight of many who had fainted or lay prostrate on the ground in an agony of conviction, was as unbelievable as it was unprecedented." Many in the meetings laughed out "with sheer joy, on their feet or standing on the pews." On one occasion, the leader, Evan Roberts, felt directed to take up a special offering for foreign missions: "The money could not be counted because of the powerful impressions which overcame the congregation."[2]

These are the views and assessments of those on the *outside*, spectators, as it were. Those on the *inside*, the participants, saw things in a different light. A Baptist minister, the Reverend R. B. Jones, became convinced of "the great need to be filled with the Holy Spirit." He aligned himself with some of the revival leaders, believing that "there is a tide in the order of God. If we are caught in the flood, we shall be blessed with great success in our work." Three weeks into the meetings, he penned this testimony to the great personal blessing he experienced in Llandrindod, Wales, in 1904:

I am, thank God, out in the light with you. At last I am able to exercise that simple faith and

[2] Evans, pp. 90, 92, 109.

trust in God's promises and truth. This power has been given me to overcome numerous temptations. Oh, how sweet it is to pray! What a wonderful book the Bible has become! Formerly, it was a collection of texts, now its every word is fraught with a message to me personally. Wherever one turns on receiving this experience, one is filled with the wonder of it all, and is not the greatest wonder received when one thinks that he was contented to be so long without it, and how wonderfully simple it is—Jesus living in me? In consequence of my self-surrender to Him, I am His and He is mine... I have simply to repeat and plead His promise and trust Him to get me through safely and Lo, it is done!... *I am waiting for more and there is more, more, and more.* Oh, for a life of thorough dependence upon the Lord and great faithfulness to His will![3]

It's hard to find fault with such a testimony, for these are the issues of the heart, and represent core Christian values and priorities. With similar focus, the revival scholar Iain Murray brings the following reflections to bear on testimonies from a period fifty years earlier, during the Second Great Awakening; though there is a lapse of time, the assessment serves as an evaluation not only of the Welsh testimonies, but of those of our day, as well:

[3] Evans, p. 32; emphasis added.

They awoke to a life not new in kind, but new in degree, and in all truth and soberness a new prospect opened before our Church and country. If revival is a larger giving to the church of grace already possessed—a heightening of the normal—then it follows that the evidences by which revivals are to be judged are the same as those which form the permanent evidences of real Christianity. Foremost in the New Testament list is the evidence of love to God and men.[4]

With Murray's evaluations in hand, we look to some who have recorded the work of grace that they have experienced in this outpouring, with specific consideration given to their experience of prayer and their praying for others. As in *Catch the Fire*, the following testimonies are first-person accounts, and have been edited only for syntactical purposes. All the testimonies have been released for publication with permission. Three of the original testimonies from *Catch the Fire* are updated; roughly a year has elapsed since these folk recounted their experiences.

* * *

Belma Vardy
Belma has a very effective dance and worship ministry.
Travelling extensively, she works with adults, teens, and
children of many different denominations, teaching them

[4] Murray, p. 24.

157

how to know a greater intimacy and freedom with God. She has produced four worship dance videos: God's Children in a Celebration of Dance, Discipling Children in Worship Dance, Devotional Dance, *and* Let's Dance!

In *Catch the Fire*, I shared some of my testimony of the ways in which I experienced the power of God's love in my life. There were many other things taking place that I did not, and at the time could not, convey. It is an honour and a privilege to be able to share more of God's grace in my life in these few pages.

For weeks I had been going to the meetings at the Airport Vineyard. All around me, people were manifesting the Spirit's presence and power in all sorts of ways, but nothing seemed to be happening to me. I wanted so badly to have what the others were getting. I prayed and prayed. Nothing happened. I was really starting to feel quite strange about this. I started to ask God questions. "What was wrong with me? Why aren't You touching *me*? Have You forgotten about me?" I would sit quiet as a mouse at the meetings and just take it all in, sometimes really focussing in on some of the manifestations. I continued to come to the meetings, watching, waiting, and wondering. One evening during worship, I just hung my head and prayed in tongues. All of a sudden, I felt something that can only be described as a liquid heat rise up from the inside of me, and through all the music and singing I heard God's Voice in a loud whisper saying, "I want you to worship Me. I want you to seek Me."

I raised my hands and felt His Presence wrap around me. I repented for not seeking Him first, but rather the manifestations. That night I discovered some of what it means to meet God face to Face.

The next day I was walking through a department store. At the same time, I was praying quietly under my breath, thanking the Lord for the intimate time of worship we had enjoyed together the night before. All of a sudden I found myself in the middle of the store's toy section. My instinct was to run, as I had wanted to many times before. But instead, I found myself glued to the floor. I stood in silence and looked around. I was shocked! I realized my heart wasn't reeling. The deep ache I'd carried for seven long years was gone! I gasped in amazement. Tears started to roll down my face.

I need to explain a bit of my past. After twelve years of marriage, my husband walked out on me. That devastated me, ripped apart my emotions, and left me feeling crushed, broken-hearted, and overcome with grief. I was even more wasted when, a few months after he left, I found out that he was living with another woman, and that she was carrying his baby! This completely did me in. Hopelessness, despair, and anxiety-filled days were followed by lonely nights with endless hours of weeping. The hurt took deep root, and eventually became anger; the anger became bitterness, and a dark depression set in.

Different fantasies would run through my mind. For a while, I wanted to kill my ex-husband and his girlfriend, Noreen,[5] kidnap their baby and run away. That was supposed to be *my* baby.

When I heard they were having another child, I felt I was on the edge of a nervous breakdown. I shuddered whenever Noreen came to mind; the anger and hate became stronger, and tormented me for almost six years.

It was for these reasons that I had such a hard time in a toy store. Baby clothes, baby toys, diapers, etc.— they all stirred up a hurt that was just too deep to bear.

But here I found myself standing in the middle of this toy section. This time there was *no* pain, *no* heartache, *no* sadness. I asked myself, "Where did all that stuff go?? It's gone!" The realization dawned that no one but the Lord could bring this healing. This was truly a miracle of God! He had completely washed away all my pain.

As I stood there glued to the floor, I started to thank Him and praise Him, and as I did so, I felt joy bubble up from the inside of me. That same feeling of liquid heat poured all over me again, bringing with it a feeling of total peace. The thought came to me, "Lord I want to follow only You and what You have for me. You may have purposed the shaking or laughing for others, but for me You choose to work differently, and I accept that."

A number of days went by. As I was having my devotions and praying in the Spirit, I felt a longing to

[5] This is not her real name.

pray for Noreen. This really shocked me, and I found it very strange as I had never done that before. But I was feeling a love and compassion for her that I knew could come only from the Lord. As I started to pray for her, these feelings became stronger and more real. Again I felt that liquid heat!

Over the next few days, I continued to feel compelled to pray for Noreen, and at one point, I heard a whisper. It seemed to come from the inner depth of my soul. But it also seemed to fill the room. The voice said, "Call Noreen." At first I thought I was imagining it. I continued to pray, this time in tongues, trying to ignore the voice. It became louder and I felt it tugging at my heart. I thought, "This *can't* be."

I waited. Two weeks went by. I did not call. But the tug on my heart continued, and it wouldn't go away. I just could not get up enough nerve to call. I rehearsed my excuses, and the best I could come up with was "What could I possibly say to her?" One morning, while wrestling all this through again in prayer, the Lord answered back, "I will give you the words. Trust Me."

A month later, I was praying again—and felt myself being overcome by His Presence. I picked up the telephone and dialled. I started feeling very nervous and wanted to get off the line before she picked up. Noreen came on the telephone, and I didn't identify myself, but just shared with her some things that were on my heart. Noreen listened and then she thanked me. I was about to hang up when she said, "Wait! Do you know how I can get hold of Belma?" I felt myself tightening up and very curtly asked, "Why?" Noreen answered, "Because I have got to tell her I am so sorry!"

I felt my heart completely soften and melt. Tears rolled down my face. Suddenly I felt the Presence of the Lord even more intensely, as if He was flowing through the telephone wires. I identified myself to Noreen, and the conversation that followed lasted for three and a half hours that night! We spoke again the next day for another three hours! We called each other for the next two weeks almost every day. I felt a love and compassion for this woman that I knew could only come from God. She was now alone with her children and was struggling to make ends meet. I was able to share my faith in God with her. Another miracle from God.

Four weeks went by, and though I stopped calling, I continued to pray for Noreen on a daily basis. Once again I felt a tug on my heart. During one of my prayer times, I saw what the Lord wanted me to do next. In my spirit, I saw a picture of my car filled with groceries and clothes and toys for Noreen and her children. I believed that this picture could only be from God, so I proceeded getting busy shopping. It took six weeks to get all the things together. I felt totally led by love to do this. I prayed over every item and every article. When it was all ready, I called Noreen and arranged to meet with her.

We met on a Sunday morning in a church parking lot. At first it felt extremely awkward and we both seemed quite nervous. I prayed under my breath. Suddenly I felt the heat again, and I sensed the Presence of the Lord with us. From that moment on I felt an atmosphere of total peace and I knew that this time together was in God's perfect will! I then asked Noreen to open up her trunk. I started to fill it with groceries. Noreen began adding up the dollar value of the bags and said, "I'm going to have to pay you back for all of this." I said, "No, I don't want you to pay it back. Just receive it as a gift." The bags continued to go into her trunk until it was completely filled. Noreen then started to help me load more bags into the back seat of her car and then the front seat, until the car was so full we couldn't get another thing in. Noreen started to cry and said, "No one has ever done anything like this for me before. Why are *you* doing it?" I answered her, "Because it's in my heart to do." She asked, "But what will I tell my children?" I answered, "Just tell them that God cares for them." Noreen just shook her head and said, "I feel like I'm in another world."

We ended up talking in the parking lot for an hour—the first time we'd spoken face to face. Towards the end of that time, I gave Noreen a Christian video for her children, and then we said our good-byes. I felt her heart open as she gave me a long, eight-second hug. I felt like we were surrounded and immersed in so much love. The love of Jesus.

As I drove away, prayers of thanksgiving gushed forth for miracle after miracle. All of a sudden I felt a heat fill the car, and then, in my spirit, I saw a picture.

Noreen, her children, and I were standing in the throne room of God in front of the Father. Jesus was standing behind us, with His Arms on both our shoulders and what looked like wings of protection hovering over the children. I clearly heard a loud whisper fill my car as He said, "Those children do not belong to Noreen, they belong to Me. And whatsoever you have done to them, you have done to Me." I started to weep and intercede for their salvation. I knew that God had His Hand on them.

* * *

God has healed and restored my broken heart. He has washed away my grief, hopelessness, and despair, my anger and bitterness, and He has replaced it all with His unconditional love and His peace. I know that when we harbour anger and bitterness, we only destroy ourselves and put up walls that keep us from receiving from God. I have found that as I respond in prayer, and in trusting obedience walk out the desires of God's heart, the walls I have put up start slowly collapsing. As they come down, I'm far more able to hear a lot more clearly from God. It has been a privilege and an honour that God used me in this way to show my forgiveness and God's Love towards Noreen.

* * *

I continue to go to the Airport Vineyard for the nightly meetings. I just sit and soak in His presence. Still no major physical manifestations on the outside, but what's been manifested on the inside of my heart leaves me grinning as those around me shake and fall over laughing. In my times alone in prayer with God, just loving Him and seeking Him, He makes Himself so very real to me and shows me His thoughts and His ways. It is in those times that I realize how deeply God has worked at changing my heart. Recently I realized that through all of this, I've been given the opportunity to act on the Scripture in John 12:32, where Jesus says: "[A]nd I, if I be lifted up from the earth, will draw all men unto Me...."

*   *   *

I serve on the ministry team at the Toronto Airport Vineyard two nights a week, and it, too, is a privilege and an honour. Such a tremendous love and compassion have grown in my heart. It has also made me realize how hungry people are for God, and how broken the world really is. I feel completely humbled at the thought that God would use me—to help pray for people from other nations from all over the globe.

The faith of these people coming to the Toronto Vineyard is beyond measure, and it keeps affirming me in my faith. As I see them stand in the prayer lines with their faces upward, their hands outstretched, just longing for a touch from Almighty God, I have a deep ache in my heart to see them healed and whole. I then watch as God's power, His love, His grace and His mercy pour out on them. It leaves me in awe every time.

I think of one lady who was so nervous when I asked if I could pray for her. She said she'd never been "slain in the Spirit" and absolutely did not want to do that. I assured her that she did not have to be down on the ground to receive what God had for her, that she could also receive by standing. "Good," she said, "because I want to stand all the way through it." I started to pray for her. I was standing at least eighteen inches away from her; I was certainly not touching her with my hands, just praying. No sooner had one sentence come out of my mouth, than she let out a scream and down she went! She lay there, not moving a muscle!

I continued to pray with her for a while, then moved on to pray for others. Later, I came back to her to see how she was doing, and she shared with me that she had felt such a tremendous power hit her she'd never felt anything like it! There she was, flat on her back!

As she was lying there, the Lord showed her that this was like a hospital and she was lying on the operating table, and all those people were having surgery. She saw the ministry team as the doctors and nurses, and the chief physician, Jesus, was putting His healing hand on everyone who was present. I stood there totally astonished at what God had shown her.

It is such a privilege to hear what God is doing in people's hearts! I find it a wonderment, and so very exciting! It is such a blessing for me to watch others get blessed. It makes me want to pray even more!

What I also find amazing is that so many varied

churches from different denominations are coming together to worship as one body before Him, learning to love one another and learning to serve one another. It is so exciting to see that the Toronto Airport Vineyard is having the Baptists preach, the Pentecostals, the Anglicans, and the list goes on! And even on the ministry team there are many serving who are not only from the Toronto Airport Vineyard but also from so many different denominational churches and backgrounds. It is so precious to be a part of the ministry team and to watch as God continually knits hearts together with His love.

In all of this, two verses come to my mind over and over again. One is from John 3:30, that "He must increase, and I must decrease." The other is from Colossians 2:2, that "our hearts be comforted, and knit together in love."

* * *

Alan Wiseman, May 1995
Alan is the son of missionary parents, and was raised in South Africa. He is a church musician by profession, having studied music at the University of Western Ontario, and theology at Ontario Theological Seminary. He currently serves Grace Presbyterian Church as director of worship, and is also responsible for training and equipping their prayer team. As a composer, he is currently applying his imagination to Christ's high-priestly prayer, John 17.

It has been more than one year since my first visit to the Airport Vineyard. At the time, I had no idea of the significance the visit would have on my life. Now, fifteen months later, I look back on that day as the beginning of a glorious landslide that has drastically altered the spiritual landscape of my soul—and I praise God for every pebble that He has moved! In *Catch the Fire* I testified to this new month-old work in my life. I am grateful now for the opportunity to reflect on His continued grace to me throughout 1994 and into 1995: the fire continues to burn!

Looking back over the past year, I recognize a lot of change. But the transformations I have experienced are not the sort that I went through at school when I was learning new ideas. They are not primarily in my mind, but in my heart. I have not learned something new so much as become someone new. I felt, after being prayed for at the Airport Vineyard the first time, that I had undergone some sort of spiritual operation. As in physical surgery, I was wholly ignorant of the actual procedure of this operation, yet I knew it had been successful, because I now "worked better." I continue to discover how skilful a surgeon the Lord is, especially as I find new ability and freedoms. All this is so very different from learning new lessons to be appropriated. Even the *way* I learn now is far more subjective and relational. I am being led deeper and deeper into the mystery of Incarnation, where the reality of Christ is not taught to me, but "birthed" in me.

A year ago, after my first experiences at the Airport, I wrote a song expressing some of my new experience of God's grace. In it I described my discovery that the story of my life was not really my search for God, but rather His search for me—it was not my song of invitation to Him, so much as it was His song of invitation to me. I called it "Come Love of Mine." It expressed a lesson that I thought I had learned. But in January of 1995 I went through a very difficult time. It was a time of great disappointment with people, a time of feeling very alone and uncared for, a time of seeing my own incompetence when there was simply no human help to be found. I was brought to the place of having no initiative left. It was in this time that I began to experience yet even more profoundly the knowledge that Jesus sought me, even when I had no strength to seek Him. I learned that it was much more important that I respond to His initiative in loving me rather than try to prove that I loved Him, and through this very painful time, I realized that when I wrote "Come Love of Mine," the truth of the song had only been conceived in my spirit. It has taken quite a bit more time for it to bear fruit in my life experientially.

In February my wife gave birth to a baby boy, our second; we named him Andrew. Shortly after he was born, I was holding him in my arms, and I sang "Come Love of Mine" to him. The thought occurred to me that I had never sung that song to my first-born; then I quickly remembered that this was

169

because I had not yet written it when Peter was born. I went on to think of the circumstances surrounding the writing of the song. It slowly dawned on me that the song had been finished at the same time of the year that Andrew had been conceived. How wonderful to realize that Andrew's conception, gestation, and birth coincided exactly with God's message of love to my spirit. I had conceived a song of His love, lived with it nine months, and then borne the fruit of it in my life. At the same time my wife had conceived a child, nurtured him in her womb, then given birth to a beautiful baby boy. And to complete the beauty of this outward sign of God's grace, Andrew was born on Valentine's Day!

I share these personal stories because I feel that it is important for everyone to realize that when God imparts His blessing in a time of renewal, it is not like a new possession that has been given to us. It is not a trophy to be placed on the mantel of our lives, declaring to those around us, "See, I've got God's blessing." The best gifts from God are not so much *given* to us as they are *born* in us. They are not static possessions, but living treasures that require our nurturing care. Andrew is a wonderful gift of love to us and he gives us incredible joy. In the same way God's gift of love to me is a great joy, but it is also a real responsibility.

The awakening I have experienced has been an ongoing response to God's love song sung into my spirit. I have learned a lot along the way, and I now know that I have the order of the relationship sorted out. He is the lover; I am the beloved. His is the initiative, mine the response. And, as I listen to His song, I find myself continually being changed, as more of the fire of God's love burns deeper into my soul, incarnating the life of Christ within me.

These gospel realities work themselves out in all sorts of practical ways. For instance, I was with a friend a few months ago. We bowed our heads to spend a few moments in prayer, and I immediately began to talk to myself: "I have nothing to offer ... I am feeling so low ... I don't think I have the faith to pray for someone right now ... O Lord, help me." Then, suddenly, I was filled with the realization that God wanted to minister to my friend. I felt His desire to do so. And as surely as I knew that God wanted to minister to my friend, I knew that I was the only one present at the moment—so God would have to use me! My perspective was totally transformed. It was no longer focussed on my ability to pray and believe. It was focussed on God's desire and ability to bless. I began to respond to His love and to pray for my friend out of the faith that welled up within me. As I did so I began to know more specifically just how God wanted to bless my friend, and prayed according to that end. As I spoke forth the things that the Spirit revealed, I saw God accomplish more of His will in my friend's life. These purposes were first born in my heart and then, through my prayers, they became reality in someone else's life! What a miracle—we can actually pass on the love of God that is born within us!

This revelation has not come without its struggles. One of the barriers in my understanding of this truth was a statement I heard growing up: "God loves you and has a wonderful plan for your life." While this is true, unfortunately I always saw that plan as a type of blueprint. God's will for me was like a blueprint of specific events, dates, and decisions. God's will was an external plan, and I had to do my best to discern what the specifics of that plan were so I would be sure to conform to it, so that I would please Him. This static concept of God's will has proved problematic for me because I grew to believe that God was more concerned with my ability to fulfil the events of His plan, than He was with my heart's ability to respond freely in relationship with Him.

I now see that God relates to us as Lover, not Contractor. He wants to simply *have* us, more than He wants to have us *do* something. Yes, He does will that we live a certain way and do certain things, but this is only so that His ability to love us and receive our love will be more complete. The goal is fellowship more than service. It really is as Jesus said: "I no longer call you servants, but friends."

Changing metaphors, I now see His will like a great river. It is not a plan like a map with a set course. It is more like the force of great desire that is drawn towards its end and, like a river, flows towards that end inexorably. His will, like a river, is sovereign in that it cannot be held back from reaching the ocean. It may come across impediments along the way, but these only change the route; they do not affect the destination. I find myself in the midst of that great river. I have the choice of becoming an impediment to His desire, or of being swept along in its flowing. If I resist for a time I will be left behind. I have resisted more than I like to admit, but God in His goodness has given me the opportunity of repenting of my foolishness and then throwing myself in at a later point. So I have not gone as far with the river as I might, but I do not want to be left behind anymore. I do not want to dally at the bank of the river, getting in and out with the whims of my fickle heart. I want to plunge into the depths to become part of the surge of His loving will. I want to experience the journey of His desire flowing towards its sovereign end.

As I have waded out into this river I have found not only His desire for me, but His desire for others at the same time. This passion has drastically changed my prayer life. I recently prayed, "Lord, descend into my emotions and fill me with Your desire, and align my whole being accordingly." Two days later I was walking along a major street in downtown Toronto, and as I looked at the people passing by me I was filled with love for them. I saw each person as incredibly unique and valuable. Since this outpouring, something I do repeatedly is shake with an "extraordinary epilepsy"; as I saw these people on the street, I began shaking violently with a desire to connect with them—for them to connect with each other. I had to close my eyes to diminish the shaking.

Then that very afternoon I fell into an old pattern of sin. I could not understand what had come over me. Why the sudden turn around from one extreme to another? I went to the Lord in prayer and I soon had my answer: I was afraid of His desire. It was not *His* holy passion that had led me into sin. Like Jonah of the Old Testament, God's call on my life felt as though it would overwhelm me it was so large, so deep. My sin was rooted in my fear of the passion of the call. I did not trust myself with it, and therefore I did not trust Him. In my fear I had fled from Him, but I could not flee from the passion He had given me. And so, as I fled from Him, I had perverted the love He had given me for others, and turned it into something ugly and self-serving.

In my growing up I struggled with many passions. Most of them were not godly! Most of the time, I have controlled myself with great discipline. I evaluated everything I felt, and when I discerned something suspicious, I did my best to repress it. This constant self-evaluation made me very self-conscious, and left me without real freedom to respond naturally and freely with others. I realize now that I have to let the Holy Spirit be the judge of my innermost thoughts. I have to allow Him to affirm me when I am walking in Him, and convict me when I am walking in the flesh. I need to live listening to Him, rather than watching myself, because my self-conscious analysis is a subtle form of pride that ensures that others do not see my sin, and all it has succeeded in doing is allow me to hide some of my sin and its consequences. Now I have learned that this self-conscious behaviour controls my godliness as well! I have been trying to do the Holy Spirit's job—and failing miserably at it. Rather than repressing all strong feelings, I now ask the Holy Spirit to purify them. God *desires* His will; He does not just think it. I now know that when I get into His holy river, I am going to flow with His feelings, and I am going to feel! I will not just have new ideas to carry out, but rather will have new passions to respond to. This is the wonder of Christ in me!

*   *   *

I was praying with a group of friends quite some time ago. One friend I'll call Elizabeth had been suffering with depression and negative thoughts. We surrounded her and began to pray. I did not know where to begin so I asked the Holy Spirit to teach us how to pray. In the silence of our first few seconds of waiting on God, I began to experience powerful emotions. These were so strong that I could not talk about them for some time. My shoulders began to heave with sobs as I saw Elizabeth as a tiny, new-born baby. I experienced the ways in which she struggled for her own life. At the same time I felt Christ's desire for her to live, and knew that she would live because He desired it. I experienced her anxiety, His desire, and then her gratitude all at the same time. In all of this, I knew that I was participating in Christ's healing work in her heart.

In talking with Elizabeth later, I was able to assure her that it was no happy accident that she had survived; she was alive today not because of the intervention of a nurse, but because of Christ's intervention, calling her into life through His love. I was able to convey to her first-hand, just how powerful was His love calling her into life. I knew that this love, present at her birth, was just as strong today, and that it was calling her out of her negative, self-defeating thoughts.

God loves us all into life. Allowing Him to be the lover who initiates His love in my life as His beloved has certainly changed the way I live. I now know so much more of the way He loves His children—because I not only know it, but can feel it. And I find it much easier to know His will because He imparts revelation into my heart and not just my mind. It changes the way I live and work.

For instance, I have always struggled with procrastination. Actually, I should probably just call it sloth! I find it very difficult to work hard or consistently without a great deal of outside pressure to force me to it. I often set the external deadlines myself, because I know that without them I will accomplish next to nothing. In reality I am just acknowledging to myself that my motivation to work is not internal. I need someone or something to depend on me or I will not produce. This attitude is true of my spiritual work, as well. The work I do for the Lord—prayer and service—needs lots of pressure to make me faithful to it.

When there are lots of people around depending on me to be spiritual and to lead them, I find it fairly easy to be motivated. But when the pressure is off... well, the work slows down ... and eventually ... stands still. I struggle to force myself to work out of love for the Lord. But I do not have much success. Recently, however, the light has gone on!

The Lord showed me the motivation of my heart: I work primarily to please other people. I want their approval, I want their praise, and I want their remuneration! In my devotional and spiritual work, I was relating to God like a boss who had employed me in His service. I was working to please Him. He then revealed to me that it is, in fact, impossible for me to please Him with my work. Christ alone was able to please God. He showed me that He did not want me to try to please Him with what I could accomplish anymore, that He had never intended work for that purpose. The issue is not labour but relationship.

The opportunities that God gives us for service are not given in order that we would please Him. They are given more so that we can have fellowship with Him! We serve Him so that we can be involved in what He is doing. We serve Him so we can be where He is. We get involved in His will so that we won't be left out of it. God showed me that I don't please Him by how well I do *my* work, but by how well I participate in *His* work. I please God by being found in Christ. And since Jesus always did what He saw the Father doing, we know that to be in Him is to be about the Father's business. In terms of motivation, there's a world of difference. Pleasing God, I am sad to say, never seemed a strong enough motive to keep working hard. But the new passion that I have for Him is enough to drive me on to seek more fellowship with Him. His presence is more than enough.

This new understanding brought clarity to something that has confused me the past few months. Previously, as I had grown more and more in love with Jesus, it actually became harder to work for Him. This was because when I served Him in my own strength, I actually cut myself off from His presence, and consequently the work began to feel onerous indeed. But what a joy to know that He does not want my work *for* him. Rather, he wants to accomplish His work *in* me. He wants me for fellowship, and since He is constantly about His work, the best way to spend time with Him is in doing what He is doing!

The goal of my life is not service anymore, not even service for God. It is fellowship. As I make this the goal for my daily life, it transforms and redirects my work, bringing it into the presence of God.

Even prayer is no longer spiritual "work." Now it is the open door into fellowship with God's love. It is the means of my participating in what God is doing. As I pray about what He is doing, I am doing it with Him! And when I am doing something with God, I am having fellowship with Him. Working with God in prayer not only brings me into fellowship with Him so that I can receive more of His love, it also puts me in touch with His love for others, such that I begin to know a fullness of fellowship I'd never dreamed of. As I work in prayer beside my Father, I know that I belong to Him and He belongs to me. I also know that everyone else belongs to Him, as well. I then begin to realize that I am one with all those who acknowledge Him. They are my brothers and sisters. They belong to me and I to them. I have never known love such as is found in the Father's will.

* * *

Melanie Morgan-Dohner, May 21, 1995
Melanie and her husband, Dennis Morgan-Dohner, are associate pastors at the Hopkinsville, Kentucky Vineyard. They are also psychotherapists at a Christian counselling centre. Melanie is mother to Monica—since kindergarten, Monica has had a recognized learning disability.

It has been a year since our girls were healed of dyslexia! Heather Harvey, daughter of our senior pastors, Graham and Mary Harvey, was healed during her time at the Toronto Airport Vineyard, and came home and prayed healing for our daughter, Monica. Our lives will never be the same! We have watched the girls do amazing things, and as they have changed, so have we. God's healing touch reaches in so many directions.

A learning disability affects a person's life so completely, and is shared by the whole family. Since Monica struggled with her first year of school, we have worked with her, been frustrated at her and with her, and cried for her. As a family, we had come to know that instructions would always have to be explained slowly, that signs would have to be read out loud and menus would have to be interpreted, that subtitles on a movie screen would have to be whispered and homework would require hours and hours every day. There was never a time that we weren't all being touched by Monica's inability to process symbols, letters, and numbers.

When Heather came home from Toronto, she was determined to pray for others with dyslexia, the first being Monica. Falling to the floor under the Holy Spirit, Monica got up reporting much the same story that Heather had told. Monica's first words were "I feel like I have all the pieces to my puzzle for the first time." Her dad and I didn't really know what God had done. We hoped for relief for Monica, that life would not be as hard as it had been, but we'd lived with dyslexia for a long time, and truthfully, we were prepared to keep battling it. Monica, however, felt instantly that something very dramatic had happened, and this was verified the next week by her reading tutor, who had just recently completed the testing to determine the extent of Monica's learning disability.

What was immediately evident was that Monica's brain was successfully processing what her eyes saw. The letters in each written word were now staying in the correct order for her. She could sound words out starting with the first letter. She couldn't do that before, as she normally saw the middle or ending letters as the first. For example, she would say that the word *ship* started with a "p" sound. She no longer saw letters reversed, confusing b's with d's. And when she wrote, all the letters faced the right way. Monica could sound out syllables in the right order, and move from one line of text to the next consistently, for the first time.

For the week after Heather's prayer, Monica reported each day, "I understood what was going on at school today!" She was quite amazed by it. As the days went by, she changed so dramatically that we couldn't miss it. She picked out books that interested her, and used them to learn how to read. Both Heather and Monica are scrambling to catch up some of the basics of reading, but for the first time they can, because they can finally trust what they are seeing.

Over this year, Monica has had to fight the temptation to go the easy "tell me what it says" way. When challenged, though, she reads quite well, and often says "Oh, that wasn't even hard." Last week, she was very indignant when her sister reached over to help her find the book of 1 Peter in her Bible. Her message is often "Please do not forget that I can do this myself now."

Math, too, had been a terribly difficult subject for Monica. She couldn't line up the figures properly, and with her numbers scattered all over the page, calculations were never correct. The first week after she received prayer, Monica brought home a math paper that I refer to as "Junior Accountant." It was rows and rows of perfectly shaped, perfectly spaced and lined up numbers. I was stunned by it. I knew no mere change in her thinking or in her beliefs about herself, no lifting of feelings of inadequacy, could have done that. God had worked something far beyond what I had dared to hope.

Before the end of this school year, we were invited to Monica's school to an authors' tea. Monica had volunteered to do a public reading of an essay that she had written! A little more that a year ago, this would have been an impossible dream. Yes, we cried. Yes, we realized how big a thing God has done!

As monumental and wondrous as her reading is to me, Monica receives this healing as just one part of knowing that God touched her. She felt His hand upon her, and at the same time that her brain was healed, her heart was changed forever by the knowledge that He knows her, loves her, and wants to see her free. At twelve years of age, she is filled with confidence in the Living God. She knows Him as a God who wants to help His children, who is willing and able to heal them, and who will use her to do it. Monica and Heather feel confident in asking Him to heal someone else. This is fruit that cannot be medically tested.

* * *

Heather's progress is equally as startling. In the past year, she has progressed through three grade levels in math and two grade levels in language arts. Beyond her assigned school work, she is now reading three books a week. Her parents say she is "devouring books." She is understanding both written and spoken instructions, something that was very difficult for her previously. Like Monica, she has stopped having dyslexiclike letter and word reversals, and can sound words out. She is learning difficult spelling words and remembering them. Recently Heather read aloud something in the newspaper that interested her, and her mother, Mary, Heather's mother, said she was startled. "I think it will be a long time before I get used to her just being able to read. It was such a huge problem, and now it's just gone!"

Mary says that there has been a dramatic change in Heather's self-confidence. When Heather was young, she was very determined and upbeat and seemed to charge through life. But her parents watched that get battered down by the difficulties she experienced while trying to learn. A common problem for dyslexics is that something learned might disappear and be a mystery again the next day or the next week. For Heather, this was so defeating that she stopped wanting to try new things. It seemed so pointless. Now she approaches life with gusto, and Mary feels that she is seeing her daughter's natural personality being restored.

* * *

Monica and Heather passionately understood that they were to give away what they had received. The two girls and their sisters began praying for anyone who wanted healing of a learning disability, and to everyone's joy, people began reporting healings. Word began to spread, and others came to our meetings to receive prayer. The girls accompanied us to various meetings and conferences during the year, and every time that they were asked to share their story, they ended up spending the evening praying for people.

When their story was printed in the book *Catch the Fire*, we began getting letters from people who, having read about the girls' healings, were suddenly filled with the idea that they, too, could be healed. Parents asked us to pray for their dyslexic children. Grandparents wrote and asked us to pray for their grandchildren. Some of the letters had nothing to do with dyslexia at all, but were from parents whose children had other medical and physical problems, and they also asked for prayer. It seemed that God had used our story to bring hope, faith, and excitement to people scattered all over the world. We began getting letters from England, Ireland, Scotland, Wales, Canada, Switzerland, Australia, New Zealand, and South Africa. At this point, we've received over seventy letters, and they keep coming, a few a week.

It has been a privilege to pray for all of these people. At meetings at the church, we read the letters and pray for the requests. Some of the letters have been from pastors who want God to set their churches on fire. The girls have especially loved praying for those pastors. They understand about wanting more of God. We gather around, and pray that His Spirit will be manifested in large, wonder-filled ways, lighting fires, bringing refreshing, and renewing, and passion to the churches. We pray for the lost to be drawn in.

We could tell when the book was released in the United States because instead of letters, we got mostly phone calls! In five months, we've probably prayed with eighty people, by phone. In the beginning, people would call and ask if they could put a name on our "dyslexia prayer list," and since we didn't have a prayer list, we'd say, "Can we just pray for you now?" (We have an ongoing prayer list now, so that we can continue to hold these beautiful people in prayer.) We learned that the Holy Spirit has no problem finding someone long distance, and as we prayed over the phone, we could feel that He was manifestly present and doing wondrous things. It's an incredible thing to be sensing the Holy Spirit and hear that the people we're praying for are also feeling Him and perhaps shaking or jerking or getting pictures from God. Or that they've fallen down. The people on the other end of the phone sometimes come to a point where they can no longer talk. We have learned to say, "We'll hang up now, and you just rest in the Spirit," so that the phone bill doesn't include any lengthy "out in the Spirit" time.

* * *

More light! More healing! One year after our first trip to Toronto, these are two major themes that have become integrated into our prayer life. We had long ago learned that praying for healing was a good thing to do, but our experience was that if we did it a lot, *sometimes* we would see *something* happen. We had much more faith for healing at a conference, where someone known to have anointing might call out a particular condition that they sensed God wanted to heal. In those cases, the person with the condition had to be there, and the next week we would hear things like "Oh! There was an altar call for people with bad backs, and we wished you were there to get prayer." (But since you weren't, you missed out.)

Now, through this season of renewal, we have a completely difference understanding of healing prayer. It isn't just for special times and places, and it doesn't have to come through special people.

In October, we parents travelled to Toronto for the Catch the Fire conference. We shared our story with the congregation, and during the ministry time, we were approached by more than a hundred people who were asking for the anointing to go home and pray for others they knew who were struggling with learning disabilities. But the girls weren't with us—they had stayed home in Kentucky—and we suddenly wondered if *we* had any anointing. It was always the girls who had been the ones praying for healings. Now these people were asking for something completely different. We did pray (my prayers all started with "Lord, you know that the girls aren't here ...") and found that the Holy Spirit was very present: the prayer times were powerful, with people falling down, shaking, and weeping for the trials of the children. They were feeling God's heart for those who suffer with learning disabilities. And we were learning that God would use any willing vessel to pour out His healing graces.

Soon after our return from the conference, we heard from Ed Loughran, pastor of Vineyard Christian Fellowship in Joliet, Illinois. He was one who asked for anointing to pray for healing. He told us that he had seen a backward *Z* over the head of a man in his congregation, Michael Powers. Ed thought, "That's what happens in dyslexia. The letters are reversed." So Ed prayed for healing of dyslexia. Michael said that while Ed was praying, he could feel incredible heat on his entire head, as though it were in an oven.

Michael said that before Ed's prayer, he often transposed numbers and was unable to retain or comprehend what he was reading without rereading multiple times, and that consequently he hated reading, something with which Monica and Heather really identified.

Michael now reports that he can read aloud clearly, retain and comprehend things the first time, and that he enjoys reading. The experience and healing have caused the Bible to come alive to him, and he says he "can't get enough of Jesus!" God has given him many opportunities to share the love of Jesus with others. His pastor, Ed, confirms this drive to spread the news, calling Michael a "ministry animal."

A couple from another state came to our church one Sunday, bringing their ten-year-old daughter for prayer (they have asked that her name not be used, but gladly share the story). She had severe dyslexia and an inability to do any kind of abstract reasoning.

The children gathered around, praying. They prayed that the Lord would heal her of all the emotional pain she had felt about being "stupid" or "dumb" or about not being able to understand things that it seemed everyone else could understand. They prayed that she would be able to forgive other kids who had teased her or called her names. They prayed to break off any generational ties or bondages that had been involved in the dyslexia and asked the Lord to "just fix her brain." Heather's sister, Alissa, saw a picture of God putting something into the girl's brain. Soon they were all off, playing and enjoying a church potluck meal. That night, the family began the long drive home, during which the daughter had five math word problems that she needed to work on for school. She had never been able to make any sense out of these kinds of word problems because of her difficulty with abstract thinking. But for the first time ever, she understood the problems, and could explain to her mother her reasoning in how she worked out the problems and how she chose the right numbers to use to solve the problems.

Her mother was so astounded that she had her daughter retested that next week with a WISC-R, a standardized IQ test measuring linguistic ability and hand-eye performance. The testing showed that her hand-eye coordination had dramatically increased from the previous test scores. Her mother reports that she is now able to see things without the previous distortion she had before.

Herb and Carol Rees of Cincinnati visited us one weekend, bringing their granddaughter, Lindsey Crawford. They hoped we would pray for Lindsey's learning difficulties, which we did a couple of times. Our youth group took the lead this time; they use a slightly "different" prayer style, which involves praying as a group for a while, playing for a while, and returning to prayer as one of them has another thought or idea. The play time does a lot to calm the anxiety of a child who has never met them before. With Lindsey, they first asked God to reveal any spiritual roots to the dyslexia, and to let Lindsey see herself as God saw her, instead of through a filter of pain. They prayed to break the power of shame and then cut off any words that had been used to label her as less than God made her to be. They asked the Lord to bless Lindsey with peace, and they told fear to go away. The second time she was prayed for, she fell to the ground and sensed the presence of angels ministering to her. There were prayers for healing for her brain and for all emotional wounds. They prayed against confusion and asked God to replace it with clarity. They asked Him to connect or rewire anything in her brain that needed to be.

The grandfather has subsequently told us that in the following months, her math, reading, and spelling improved, and that she voluntarily reads more. She went from being unable to read, to being on the honour roll at school. Her self-esteem and love for Jesus are at a new, more mature level.

*   *   *

Incorporated into our prayer-ministry time now is a petition for more light. Interceding for light was something God began speaking to us about right after we came home from Toronto. He kept telling us to pray, "More light!" We kept trying to make it more complex, and He kept saying, "Pray more light!"

We have learned that His light reveals things, especially what's inside us; as His light intensifies, it chases away darkness. Fears, strongholds, and sins are spotlighted. The revelation of "more light" is akin to a strong searchlight being directed into a closet. The light shows up things that we didn't know were there or had forgotten were there, things that we had stored away, things that don't "fit" anymore, things we'd get rid of if we realized they were in our closets, things that God wants us to get rid of. Rather than holding coats and shirts, this closet holds attitudes, beliefs, defences, and judgements that have kept us physically, emotionally, or spiritually damaged.

These unexamined attitudes, misbeliefs, fears, and forgotten vows keep us from the intimacy God wants with us; His light reveals that which we "clothe" ourselves in, such that we're unable to "feel" His presence and draw closer to Him. These days, we pray "More light!" a lot, and when we do, there is invariably a word, a new discerning insight, or a picture given, as God reveals deep roots of pain and fear. As we offer them up, He severs the things that have bound us—things we've known about, and things we haven't.

It sure makes counselling easier! As we pray for people, we ask God to bring light; His light brings truth; truth sets people free. Light also reveals darkness, and dispels it. In a way that never ceases to amaze us, when we "get stuck" in a ministry situation and it seems nothing is happening, no one knows what to pray next, and we pray asking for more light, God always gives it. Sometimes, the person being prayed for will say, "I just remembered something. It's probably nothing ... it seems silly ..." and the Lord will show exactly how that forgotten thing is at the bottom of the issue. Or a member of the prayer team will get a picture or a word that, when spoken out, powerfully affects the one receiving prayer, breaking loose the log jam.

For instance, a couple came for a weekend from Washington, D.C. The husband thought they had come to receive prayer for his wife's panic attacks. She said she just wanted a touch from God, that her panic attacks seemed controllable with medication. We prayed together about many aspects of their lives, and eventually the ministry focussed on the woman's anxiety. We used all of our good Vineyard interviewing questions, yet felt stuck. No one knew quite what to do, so we prayed for "more light." As we prayed that, she suddenly said, "I often think it would have been better if my brother had never been born."

She explained that her parents had told her that they hadn't wanted another child, and that they had only had her brother because *she* wanted a sibling. As a young child, she had taken on the emotional responsibility for his birth and his life. In adulthood, his life seemed "messed up" and she was sure that he was not saved. Emotionally she was carrying a burden about being responsible for the creation of someone doomed to hell, and it was smothering the life out of her. She had been in therapy with a psychologist for ten years, and this had never come up.

In the ministry that followed, many prophetic words were given about letting God take care of her brother, to put the responsibility for him in God's hands. There was a picture of a door that needed to be closed. She said she was afraid of reopening it, and wanted God to lock it. Then there was a picture given of a key locking the door, and the key was the key to her brother's heart. That was why it was important for it to be in God's hands, as only He would know how to use it appropriately.

Almost a year later, I spoke with this woman. She barely remembered the details of the ministry she received. She *did* realize that she stopped taking the medication not long after we had prayed together, and that she had not had any further panic attacks. She went on to say that her life has been taken over with "a new love affair with Jesus." She and her husband have been set on fire, and been used by God to introduce many people to the renewal. It had kept them very busy, and she said that her relationship with Jesus is "truly, the most important thing in my life. I just love to be in His presence, and worship Him, and I can do it in a way I never could before."

* * *

One of our earliest lessons on "more light" came while we were praying for our daughter Autumn's asthma. She had been outside playing, when her chest began to hurt. She made her way indoors, but soon was lying on the floor, trying to catch a good breath. We were all anxious. We had prayed many times about her asthma and her allergies, and I said that I felt we always missed something. There was a word given that what we missed praying about was perfection. The word was that as a kindergartner she could excel in everything except running races, and that she had "embraced" asthma as a way out of races. Autumn immediately felt the truth of this, though we were very surprised even by the concept. She knew it to be true. It was light for her, and as we processed this revelation, the pieces started to fit together.

It was in those early school years that a doctor had diagnosed her problem as exercise-induced asthma. Every year, I had done whatever was needed to have her excused from physical education. It was frightening to see her having trouble breathing, and she would sometimes get scared just realizing that she was somewhere without her medicine. When playing outdoors, she often had to stop long before anyone else and go inside, wheezing.

When Autumn heard the word about embracing asthma, she cried at the realization of how much it had gone on to affect her life. She saw very clearly the price she had paid. She asked God to forgive her for having held on to it, and she prayed for Him to take it away. Then she heard Him say that He would also free her from the allergies. Autumn had been very allergic to grass and tree pollens, and had gone through life with pockets stuffed full of Kleenex. Ten months later, her allergies are a thing of the past, and she has not needed any of the medication that used to be a daily affair for her.

The allergies and asthma healing became another healing "focus" that we prayed about for many. A week after Autumn was healed, I was healed. I had suffered with allergies since childhood, and for all of my adult life I had used prescription medications. I have not had any allergy medicine since that day, a year ago. We understand that we do "keep what we give away," and because we live in a heavy pollen zone, we asked who in our fellowship had allergies. We got a large response when we went to ministry. Months later, about a dozen people were testifying that they were not taking their usual medication and believed they were healed. One woman said she saw the difference clearly when she prepared her income-tax forms. She was used to declaring high medical expenses because of her allergies, but she says that being healed has enabled her to "give up my drug habit!"

* * *

Not everybody has enjoyed this. There is a cost involved in having this much light. It requires of most of us our comfort. Before, we would pray, "Draw us closer to you, Lord," without realizing that He would want to do a work in us. Things that had been well hidden, even for long periods of time, would suddenly surface and become visible or be felt. When that happens, we each face the decision of whether to deal with it and get cleansed (which draws us yet closer ...), or to run. Autumn, for instance, had to face the truth of having used asthma before she was healed. She could have decided that this truth was more painful than the asthma and turned away from what God was offering. This, sadly, is something we've too often seen, and it has been painful to watch some people run. It has been *wondrous* to watch others choose freedom.

It has also been quite funny at times. For example, a man called from England wanting prayer for his son, who had dyslexia. A specific time and date were set for prayer. A half-hour before that time, a group of people gathered and began praying. The four girls were there, also. The set time came and went, and the phone call from England never came. Finally, we just prayed with the only information we had ("Lord, please heal this man's son"). Two weeks went by, during which we occasionally wondered why they hadn't called, and then the man phoned to say, "Thank you! He's healed!" When asked why he hadn't called, he replied that he hadn't intended to, and didn't know we had expected him to. He said a group had prayed over his son at the set time and day, knowing that we would be praying, too. And the results had been so dramatic that he had to call and tell us.

It is a mighty privilege to be used by God as He brings grace, joy, and healing to His children. We laugh and cry and cheer, as His plans unfold and He sets people free. May we all be blessed with more of Him!

Hearing from God, and being around what He is doing, is more fun than anything else, and we continue to welcome questions and prayer requests.[6] We rejoice in serving a BIG, BIG GOD!

*   *   *

Mary Audrey Raycroft, May 1995
Mary Audrey is on staff at the Toronto Airport Vineyard as part of the pastoral leadership team. As a teacher and exhorter, her calling and delight are in equipping believers to function fruitfully in the Body of Christ. Along with some very able helpers, she oversees the renewal ministry teams; she also conducts a wide variety of training seminars, and facilitates a very lively women's ministry—the Deborah Company. Mary Audrey ministered internationally and interdenominationally for a number of years with Christian Services Association, a Canadian-based teaching and outreach organization, prior to her full-time involvement with the Airport Vineyard.

[6] Melanie Morgan-Dohner, Vineyard Christian Fellowship, P.O. Box 754, Hopkinsville, Kentucky 42240, U.S.A. Phone 502-885-7414. Fax: 502 886-6640.

In the early months of 1994 we often wondered why the Lord would choose our relatively unknown church as His vessel through which to pour out His Spirit in renewal and revival. Certainly it appeared to be His sovereign choice, for there had been no days of concentrated prayer, no fasting, no specific evangelistic outreaches, and no passionate crying out for revival.

As I declared these facts at a recent meeting, almost boasting of our corporate prayerlessness and lack of expectation, a woman looked at me rather sadly and declared, "Well, honey, ya'll may not have been seeking God for this, but let me tell you that thousands in the body of Christ *have been* for years!" I was thoroughly convicted of my phony humility.

Prior to renewal breaking out, the practice of intercessory prayer in the church was more on a personal level rather than a corporate one; for instance, a handful of faithful individuals were especially committed to covering members of the pastoral team on a daily basis. For several months before the outpouring began, some of us had spoken of the need for a strong intercessory base—the issue seemed to be in becoming "doers of the word and not hearers only." A few began to gather weekly to wait on the Lord for specific revelations of His will for us as His church, but they had not moved into high gear as yet. Then, when renewal began, such a sense of urgency was released. Being totally out of our experience and comfort zone, we *knew* that we had to stay very close to Him. Prayer time grew from one afternoon a week to four, with the majority of the participants coming from around the world—those who had sacrificed much to come to the renewal meetings, and who were determined to get in on all that God is doing.

It is thrilling to see an almost equal number of men as well as women interceding with "warrior" vigour, at times spontaneously shouting out the Lordship of Christ, at other times praying with tears and supplications or with awe and thanksgiving. It is so refreshing to be part of a prayer group that is freed from rote, mechanical methods. After a time of personal soul searching and repentance for any sin that would spoil fellowship with the Lord, the groups quietly wait on Him for direction. These times of precious silence are rich, for in them the intercessors hear the Lord speak to them, through the Scriptures and through "now" revelation (that "still, small voice"). Then, as the prayers become verbalized, joy and faith are released as prayer after prayer entwines with a strong unified thread of purpose and spirit. Further, as they've worked together over the months, the prayer teams have been learning to hear the Spirit's specific strategies for spiritual warfare, physical and emotional healing, stamina and protection for leaders and staff, and an overall prayer covering that is so vital for the facilitating of the renewal meetings.

Another special time of prayer has just begun at the Airport Vineyard: a number of our local congregation have been impressed to set aside a whole night for intercession. From ten o'clock in the evening Sundays to six the following morning, they gather, and committed to worship and an ever-deepening intimacy with Jesus, they seek His face, and, as the Spirit bears witness, they hear His concerns for the church.

* * *

In assessing my own personal prayer experience these days, I am so thankful that God has put such an assurance in my heart: I *know* that I am totally accepted by Him and, because of that, I know that I have the freedom to come boldly into His presence with confidence. I am living out the truths of Hebrews 4:14–16 and 10:19–23 as never before:

> Since therefore we have a great high priest who has passed through the heavens, Jesus the Son of God, let us hold fast to the faith we profess.... Let us therefore boldly approach the throne of grace, in order that we may receive mercy and find grace to give us timely help.... The blood of Jesus makes us free to enter the sanctuary with confidence by the new and living way which He has opened for us through the curtain, the way of His flesh. We have a great high priest set over the household of God; so let us make our approach in sincerity of heart and the full assurance of faith, inwardly cleansed from a guilty conscience, and outwardly washed with pure water. Let us be firm and unswerving in the confession of our hope, for the Giver of the promise is to be trusted.

*   *   *

The Vineyard approach to teaching people about God's Father heart, and the call to intimacy with our Lord, has laid a wonderful foundation for our prayers and communion, i.e., communication, with Him.

I honestly feel, without presumption, that I walk in a "now" relationship with my Lord. In Him "I live and move and have my being,"[7] and communication with Him, i.e., prayer, is more of a spontaneous speaking, sharing, and listening fellowship than it is a specific set and disciplined time each day, while not negating those specific times for worship and inter- cession. I love the spontaneity that comes with that moment-by-moment walk—the listening for His voice and ideas; the frequent awareness of His cau- tions and no's; the words of knowledge and wisdom that I am learning to recognize more quickly; the joy of watching these words facilitate ministry; the fre- quent reminders that His agendas and plans are far more efficient than mine. I am finding myself turning to Him so much more frequently over these past months; I am so much more aware of His presence as I drive my car, or sit with a cup of coffee at the kitchen table, or cuddle my pup, or even dig through the paper pile on my desk! Be it on my awakening in the morning, or browsing through a shopping mall, or sharing heart to heart with friends, co-workers, and

[7] Acts 17:28.

the wonderful brothers and sisters in the Lord who pour into our church for a special meeting with the Holy Spirit, I have a stronger and longer-lasting sense of the Lord's presence than I've ever known.

As Jesus Christ ministers so obviously to us these days, we are continuously challenged to walk more and more in and after the things of the Spirit. I believe the truth of His words in John 10:1–5, that as His sheep we hear His voice above all others; this is becoming a greater reality for the Body of Christ, and it's not just theory!

* * *

In September 1994, we began to have ministry-team training sessions specifically for those who would pray for those at the nightly meetings. These are all-day workshops for new members and those who would like to apply for service on the team. At these sessions expectations, guidelines, and pointers on how to minister are presented and discussed. At the workshops several people have discovered that for any number of reasons, this kind of ministry may not be what God is calling them to. Others work through the training, and some are eventually recruited.

We also hold ongoing training sessions each Wednesday evening in the upper level of the church while the renewal meeting carries on in the main sanctuary. These sessions include a biblical foundation, from which the ministry team learns to recognize and operate in the gifts of the Spirit.

It took a while, but we have realized that the Airport Vineyard is often regarded as a model for ministry by pastors and churches around the world who are learning to administer renewal services. We tend to be closely observed for our ministry style. Therefore, we attempt to minister with God's anointing and fruitfulness in all humility, trying to avoid extremes in behaviour and style.

It is expected that each individual on the nightly ministry teams will arrive for preservice prayer already built up in faith. The half-hour prior to the renewal meeting is spent in encouraging and blessing one another—as well as asking for the Lord's specific anointing upon the worship team, the evening speaker, and those coming to receive a touch from God.

*   *   *

The purpose for the renewal ministry team is to cooperate with the moving of the Holy Spirit as God's love is poured out, restoring and empowering those who come to meet with Him night after night. It is hoped that each team member will have a servant's heart and the desire for an ever-increasing intimacy with God. The Lord has been quite definite with us that we are to protect, value, respect, care for, and edify those who come to be blessed at the renewal meetings. We realize that overenthusiasm must be tempered with much grace and self-control, knowing that God wants the best for His people. We try to ensure that insensitivity, pride, or careless words have no part in any of the ministry that is received at the Airport Vineyard. We try to instil in the team members the consciousness that being a participant in what the Holy Spirit is doing is an awesome privilege, not a right or a sign of spiritual superiority.

To this end, we encourage ministry team members to apply seriously David's prayer of Psalm 139:23–24: "Search me O Lord, and know my heart, and see if there is any offensive way within me...." One major emphasis of the pastoral leadership at the Airport Vineyard is in giving godly character first-place priority, even over and above "spiritual giftedness."

Over the months we are seeing an increase in team members' sensitivity to discern God's heart and desire towards the individual receiving prayer, and with it a heightened awareness of the individual's own state at the moment.

After all these months of ministry, night after night, week after week, there is increased encouragement for all team members to receive much "soaking" in the Lord's presence for themselves so that what they do does not become a "works" program but something that still flows from joy and delight in doing His will. An ever-increasing challenge is presented to walk free from complaining, murmuring, and criticism, for we know that it *is* the pure of heart who continue to receive ongoing revelations of the Father, as Jesus said in Matthew 5:8.

By way of some specifics, we encourage the team to pray biblical prayers, i.e., those based on the Word and the heart of God, and in that, to let prophetic blessings flow within the Apostle Paul's guidelines of "edifying, exhorting, and comforting."[8] We admonish our teams to be especially diligent in not bringing words of correction or direction.

The revival meetings do not provide, generally, opportunities for in-depth ministry involving inner-healing counselling or deliverance. It is for this reason that we encourage visitors to seek in-depth deliverance and inner-healing ministry in their home settings, as we feel that it's impossible to give appropriate pastoral follow-up in these cases. This being the "rule," we often find that the Holy Spirit sovereignly brings wonderful restoration as He ministers grace to people's hearts. Hundreds have given testimonies about God's faithfulness and healing while they have rested in His presence.

While one may think that the ministry team would be quite experienced after many months of practice, in reality we realize more than ever that each situation is unique, each person is precious and unique, and that the Holy Spirit does "custom" work in each and everyone of us. The necessity of leaning wholeheartedly on Him keeps us on our faces, for we know we absolutely cannot rely on our own understanding or ability! This is hitting home as never before.

[8] 1 Corinthians 14:3.

As Christians continue to arrive from around the world, it's becoming very clear to us that if we were ministering out of our own strength, we would soon run dry and fail. It's only through the continuing infilling and healing of the Holy Spirit that we can keep on ministering in God's love night after night and month after month. It's only by ministering from the overflow of the Spirit in our lives that we are able to keep giving.

It is absolutely the most marvellous privilege to be in this place where we can actually see the Lord manifest His grace, compassion, and restoring love as He touches hearts day after day. At times, there is a longing to know of the good fruit being produced in people's lives as a result of being in His presence and the prayer ministry given; however, we are assured and confident that He who has begun a good work in all of us will go on developing it until the day of Jesus Christ (Philippians 1:6).

* * *

Dwayne Heppner, B.Th., LL.B., M.B.A. (earned degrees in theology, law, and business.)
Dwayne is a member of the Ohio Bar Association and has worked in advertising and product management for a Fortune 100 company. Dwayne and his family joined the Toronto Airport Vineyard Fellowship in the spring of 1994, several months after the first outpourings of renewal began. He joined the ministry team in August 1994; as of March 1995, his wife, Jennifer, also serves on the team. They have three children under five years of age.

I went to the Airport Vineyard reluctantly, secretly feeling that the words *Vineyard* and *renewal* (when used in the same sentence) translated into the emotional excesses of weird people. I certainly did not think that I needed to flop on the floor or to laugh hysterically to enhance my Christian walk. The thing was, I could not deny the obvious fruit of the Holy Spirit in the lives of some of my closest friends who had recently attended the renewal meetings. I mean, these folks had been changed—rather, set free—almost overnight. By contrast, previous years of Christian counselling had been unable to effect changes in them at such a fundamental level. I had to know if this was a divine fluke or if God really was visiting the Toronto Airport Vineyard Christian Fellowship in a uniquely powerful, real way. These friends persistently invited me to go with them, so one evening I did.

The kind of behaviour I observed my first night there was only slightly bizarre. Some folks laughed loudly and long; some fell or slid out of their chairs to the floor; others had what appeared to be seizures. As a lawyer by training and disposition, I confess that my thoughts were about personal-injury liability. I was running a courtroom trial in my head, trying to determine if the church was negligent in causing bodily harm. On the other hand, for the defence, I wondered if these were acts of God or acts consented to by those manifesting the behaviour. In my mind, the jury was hung.

What *did* impress me was the way most people sang with greater passion than I had previously seen in a Christian context. In my heart I thought such manifestations of praise seemed fitting. To me, Jesus merits more cheers and adoration than the local hockey team, but I personally had never expressed myself with such passion. I had only thought about it.

My personal testimony of what God has done (and is doing) with me through the renewal meetings is long and complicated, but I won't go into a lot of detail. When I first went to Airport Vineyard, I thought that, if anything, I only needed my Christian character polished up a bit. Mostly I came to observe. *Perhaps* I might get some blessing like a promise of financial success or career advancement. Maybe it would just be a nice "experience" that would reassure me I was the kind of guy God was glad to have for an adopted son. The blessing, no doubt, would be apprehended cognitively, intelligibly, and would conform to my already sanctified (or sanctimonious) knowledge of God.

In many ways, I loved being in control of my life. I liked rallying truth and facts to support my perceptions of reality. I prided myself on using solid thinking based on hard facts, reasonable assumptions, and my razor-sharp intuition. On some intelligence tests I ranked in the ninety-seventh percentile, and by nature processed the world around me on intellectual terms. I saw no real conflict between faith and reason (and still do not, though my reasoning has expanded substantially) as long as faith was reasonable. I believed faith was my cognitive agreement with the reasonableness of God's will, as it is revealed in Scripture. But in my Christian walk, I was accustomed to powerless prayer expressed as wishful thinking. I believed God could supernaturally intervene on occasion but I generally believed that He liked working through Bible reading and sound mental processes. To put it bluntly, I lived as though I had a very small God who needed my help in some areas; He was willing to trade me for His help in other areas. I "held to a form of godliness but denied its power." I had no idea how big God really is.

I got a hasty baptism in the supernatural power of God.

My first personal experience of a physical manifestation of the Holy Spirit's presence and power happened during the worship time, about my third or fourth meeting. While we were singing, I felt a pressure on me to bend over backward. This is not for me a normal physical posture. At that time no one was praying for me, and no one had "laid hands" on me. I wondered if it was God, but got no answer. I stood my ground, and the feeling of pressure went away. When someone came to pray for me at the end of the meeting, however, I felt like I was being bent over backward again. There was nothing for my mind to process; in fact, I had no cognitive reasoning or understanding for any of the manifestations. The only evidence I had that any of it was God was that I knew *I* was not faking it, nor was I under delusion.

The effects of receiving prayer that night came well after the meeting when some of my habits began changing. For example, my wife observed that my driving had improved. I was not lane changing as quickly, I kept to the speed limits, and my choice of verbal descriptives for other drivers had changed substantially. (Just for the record, I had not intentionally set upon a program to rehabilitate my driving; it merely happened.)

It was several meetings before I actually ended up on the floor or laughed or had any manifestation similar to those testifying in the nightly interviews. When I did my first "carpet time," I remained fully conscious and lucid. I even debated with myself on the way down whether I was faking it or not.

But then I discovered I could not get up. I wanted to, I felt that I ought to be able to, I intended to, but I couldn't.

It irritated me slightly that no one seemed to notice my predicament. What's more, the person praying for me turned and went to pray for someone else. I was left to struggle with an invisible Mack truck on my chest, while God delighted in not explaining anything to my mind. On this occasion, I felt physical stirrings in my chest, which were at first quite painful, but I had no one to interpret them for me.

Time passed, and I was praying that God would fill me with His Holy Spirit and do whatever He wanted to do, just as John Arnott had instructed us to pray. As I was splayed out on the floor, my three-year-old daughter came and plopped herself across my tummy, stuck a lollipop in my mouth and asked, "Daddy, is Jesus filling you up?" I looked at her smiling face full of genuine curiosity, and managed a slight nod. Satisfied, she retrieved the lollipop and went back to playing with her sister nearby. God continued doing whatever He was doing, seemingly uninterrupted by my daughter's conversation.

After several hours, I had the strangest sensation of peace and love and of being numb on the inside. I wanted to laugh and cry, but I hadn't the foggiest idea why. Then it dawned on me—or God spoke to me— that God really did like me. It wasn't as if I'd felt unloved prior to this, but now I *felt* God's love more intensely. I realized that my emotions had been reconnected and made alive, and I could now feel intense emotions. I suppose surgery is the best metaphor to describe this "floor time." Before this experience I habitually intellectualized feelings, often holding them in a buffer zone until they could be processed. Now I was connected directly to my emotions and I felt them deeply. I had an intense awareness of and desire for God. I loved Jesus, I was quickly growing to like the Holy Spirit, and I wanted more; much more.

I should mention that the person praying for me had asked God to "heal my heart," and did so without my even saying so much as a word to him or being aware of such a need in my life.

After several months of attending meetings, I was positively in love with my Heavenly Father, wanting more of His presence in my life. He has honoured that desire, but it has come with a condition. I have to give away what I've already received. God made it clear that He wanted me to start praying for others, and I took that to mean "join the ministry team."

So I started by helping one of the prayer team members. I would stand behind the person being prayed for and, if that person "relaxed" under the Spirit's presence and needed to greet the carpet, I would assist him or her on the journey down. Then I'd pray silently or quietly under my breath, and would try to listen to what the ministry team person was praying. Usually the prayers were simple entreaties: for God to fill the person with His love, to refresh them, to bless them. Occasionally the prayer would be something like "Give them a heart of flesh; take away the heart of stone" or other biblical expressions.

On one occasion I assisted a prayer team member who spoke very specific prayers to the various persons receiving prayer. She told one person about a particular childhood event, and that Jesus was present *now* to take the pain and trauma of that event away and to minister forgiveness.

The sudden impact on that person hearing those words was unforgettable. He collapsed in tears, let out an anguished cry, and then began laughing a deep, wholesome, infectious laugh. As I looked at him, I thought I saw steel bands snapping off of his chest. The bands were not visible, but I perceived them all the same. I marvelled at this ministry team member's gifts, and secretly asked God if I could do what she was doing. The affirmative answer was not long in coming.

As that evening's ministry time progressed, I got clearer and clearer sensations for the various people receiving prayer. One fellow seemed not to be entering into worship at all, as if he was having a hard time with what was going on. The ministry team member I was catching for asked if this guy wanted prayer, and he said he did. As I took up my position behind him and gently touched his back, I suddenly felt anger and pain, situated, as it were, in *my* lower back. It increased while the prayer team member prayed, until I finally risked saying something. I leaned over and told the prayer team member about the anger and pain I was experiencing. I said also that I felt this man was struggling with bitterness, and needed to forgive whoever it was who had hurt him. The ministry team member listened, thought about it, then asked if I would pray for this man while the two of them listened. I agreed. When I told the man what I was sensing, he went a bit blank, then started to cry (something I doubt he had done in a long time). We led him in a prayer confessing his bitterness and then forgiving the offender, who, we found out, had caused an injury to this man more than a decade earlier. He told us he had been suffering from lower back pain ever since. A few moments later the sense of pain left me and *he* reported that his back was pain free! He stood there praising God, entering into the worship songs with abandoned zeal.

I have not seen this man before or since that evening so I cannot testify to a physical healing. I can only testify to the strong mental and physical impressions I had, and then to the corresponding phenomena demonstrated by this man. I don't know why the prayer team member did not sense what I sensed. We didn't get a chance to debrief this prayer time; we simply moved on to the next people. But somewhere in the deep reaches of my consciousness, I was aware of God's pleasure. It felt similar to how I feel when one of my children does what she knows is right, without having been asked.

For a while I enjoyed just "catching," and occasionally chimed in with my observations. Initially, if I spoke at all, I would first share my perceptions with the ministry team member. Sometimes he or she would use what I said, sometimes not. Together, we were testing my "knowings" to see if they were valid, accurate, and God sourced. If they were used, the prayer recipient would often be so kind as to validate what I said with an immediate manifestation—crying, falling, laughing, shaking, dancing, making loud noises, or whatever else. Although the ministry team members were instructed not to place too much emphasis on the manifestations, it was hard for me not to consider a demonstrative manifestation as somehow validating me in my gifting. It felt wonderful to pray and to have God answer in front of my eyes; and believe me, I learned to pray with my eyes open!

The Airport Vineyard ministry team has some fairly

rigorous requirements of its team members (for which I am very grateful). New recruits are helped and healed in their own walk with the Lord, and everyone on the team is encouraged to receive as much personal prayer ministry as possible. Training and supervision are provided, and required, and one must specifically be released to pray solo.

Now, not every ministry team member operates in the prophetic and revelatory gifts; those who do try to be wise and cautious risk takers. The Airport Vineyard is blessed to have outstanding pastors, teachers, and an abundantly capable ministry team director, who together provide much sound teaching and protective covering. While they are on a steep learning curve like everyone else, these saints nevertheless encourage us to press on into God and to actually use the gifts the Holy Spirit is giving. The mandate is to go for God and do what He wants, with the caveat that personal dignity will likely be sacrificed. Yeah, right!

I thought Joel's prophecy about God pouring the Holy Spirit on all flesh, etc., was nice reading. Nice, that is, until I got my first bona fide prophetic vision. Of course, the vision itself had to be a little flaky, right? Weird objects doing unusual things. No neat and tidy picture of Jesus for me, uh-uh—this vision was about ... cows—dairy cows, to be precise.

Now I had a problem. I was standing in front of a man who looked every inch a man's man. Not a hair out of place. Steel-carved biceps straining at the cotton polo shirt sleeves. His posture was ramrod straight, and I was thinking, he must have commanded a marine platoon in Vietnam or maybe an air force squadron. He was about the last guy I would want to make a fool of myself in front of, and I certainly didn't want to offend him. I found myself musing, "He probably thinks this whole Airport Vineyard thing is right off the wall, and after he hears what I feel I have to say, his suspicions will be confirmed. That's it; it's going to be all over the newspapers; we're toast, and I've scuttled the Second Coming."

As my anxiety went boldly where no man has gone before, I wondered, "What do I do with the cows I'm seeing? Do I tell him about them—do I act on this "vision"? Or do I ignore it? What will he think about God and this renewal when he hears what I have to say? Am I crazy? Is this the product of my imagination ... or of indigestion? Is it true? Is it relevant? What if I am mistaken? Did I really see what I just saw? What does it mean, anyways? Did I get the whole picture? Oh God, Oh God, Help! Oh God!"

While standing there, I analysed this nonanalysable thing, trying to keep my sanity. "No, this isn't the product of my imagination or of indigestion. It's not likely from the enemy—the cows are far too serene. It's not going to promote my personal interests if I disclose this thing to him—quite the contrary! I will, however, be unable to prove the things whereof I speak and, *therein lies the rub*. (I imagined the opposing attorney jumping up and shouting "Hearsay," "Facts not admitted in evidence," "Speculation." He then calls for a conclusion ... and the judge orders me to undergo a psychiatric assessment.)

I dismissed the fantasy courtroom and got back to my reasoning. Since this vision was not likely from me or the enemy, it must be from God. Since it came while praying for this man, it might just relate to him. Since I didn't know him and I was not likely to run into him ever again (wrong), why not go for it?

A new set of problems. I knew that the opening line was going to be crucial. I searched for the right phrase, leaned closer to his ear (no point in being overheard by anyone), and asked him, "Do cows mean anything to you?" Just at that moment, the worship music in the background ended. I felt one hundred eyes click my direction. I imagined tape recorders being turned on. The marine's eyes were closed in pensive prayer ... the silence was physically painful ... and then he answered, "Yes, they do." I went for broke. "I see dairy cows, lots of them, and they are doing ... that is, um ..." and I related the rest of what I saw in the vision. He smiled, eyes still closed. Then a big grin broke out across his face and he nearly shouted "Hallelujah." He effused thank-yous to God, intensely and repeatedly. His eyes were moist as he opened them. He shook my hand, nearly crushing it, and then went and sat down in a chair.

"That's it?" I asked God. "No explanation, no further revelation?" "You're kidding me, right?" "Hello?"

Two days later I saw this man again, and he was as relaxed as one of my visionary dairy cows on Valium.

He walked over to me, crushed my hand again, and stated confidently that "God is here at Airport Vineyard." Furthermore he said, "You will never know the significance of what you prayed [shared] with me the other day. It was a turning point in my life. By the way, would you mind praying for my wife?"[9]

* * *

As I am gaining experience "interceding in the Spirit," I find that it's both terrifying and exciting. The Holy Spirit moves quickly, deftly, and at a lively pace that challenges me to keep up. He rarely gives me a complete revelation of anything with time to ponder, but requires me to give it out as He goes along. He does, however, work at a unique pace with everyone to whom He ministers, and I am learning to keep in stride.

Some nights the ministry time moves rapidly with many words of knowledge, prophetic utterances, and impartation of gifts, healings, etc. Other nights I feel as though I come up short. One such evening I was praying general "Bless you" prayers and not getting anything specific for anyone. While some were undoubtedly receiving from God, I had no witness in my spirit that any anointing was flowing through me. I was tempted to analyse what the problem might be, but I had come to the place where I knew that the Holy Spirit's movements could not be subjected to

---

[9] Dwayne *still* doesn't know what the cows mean!

mere reasoning. There were too many variables that were beyond observation and analysis. So I continued to pray general prayers, hoping they would be effectual, until I stopped in front of one man.

He looked every inch an English vicar. He was. But I deduced that not, shall we say, by the Spirit, but from his white shirt and tie, penny-loafer leather shoes, and the English cut and look of his clothing. His face had the tired expression of so many leaders I have seen filing into the Airport Vineyard. Pastors one week away from pitching the whole business to go sell life insurance, or perhaps letting someone collect on theirs.

He courteously kept his eyes closed as I faced him for prayer, my thumbs pressing his palms, my fingers on the back of his hands. I asked whether—rather told him—he was a pastor. He hmmed. I began praying that Jesus would take all the criticisms off him, refresh him, and show him His love for him. He hmmed again; the sigh betrayed this was the same old thing all over. I waited and stared at the top of his forehead. "God, please reach this man," I thought, "lift the pain and fatigue off him." I looked down at his shoes; I looked behind him to the man waiting to catch him; I looked across the crowded room to see if the Spirit was moving on anyone else. "Father," I thought, "please ..." and I waited. Should I move on to the next man? Maybe this guy needs to "soak" awhile. I could come back later; or maybe another team member would have better "luck" with him. Nope. I waited. I half expected this man to open his eyes, smile politely, say thank-you, and give me an easy out. Nope. I waited.

For those who were never at the original Airport Vineyard facility, it may be hard to imagine people packed shoulder to shoulder, waiting to receive prayer. The main room was invariably hot and usually stuffy; the music was loud, and everyone else's manifestations were obvious and sometimes distracting. Clear floor space was always at a premium, and often the carpet behind someone got occupied before he or she could drop onto it. Ministry team members were frequently more concerned with keeping people out of harm's way (from falling bodies) than they were with praying for someone. The practical needs of the moment meant that prayer team members had to move quickly to those manifesting most dramatically, secure them, and then return to pray for others who manifested less dramatically. Spending a long time praying for one person was a luxury, especially if it didn't appear that anything spiritually significant was happening.

I can't say exactly how long I waited with this vicar. It felt like a *long* time. I looked at him and prayed silently, not really saying anything to God, just trying to tune in to Him. Then, as I looked at the Vicar's face, I seemed to see something up over my head, off in space about a mile. I zoomed in for a closer look, and saw a massive, ancient structure, almost square, that dated, I guessed, from the early Middle Ages. A flash of light came out of it or towards it; the walls came crashing down, and it was virtually razed to the ground. Next, I saw Jesus, not clearly, but I knew it was Him, and He was dancing around the ruins. In their place, a new fortress was raised up. It became a stronghold of righteousness, a bastion of joy, and the Prince of Peace took up residence there. The darkness all around began lifting, and power and righteousness went out from that place to all England. The angelic beings who took up their positions on the west, north, and south walls were the biggest warriors I had "seen" to that time.

After the cow deal with my marine, I had considerable confidence in the pictures the Lord showed me, so I shared this one with the vicar. (I've omitted much and changed a detail or two to protect confidentiality.) Suddenly it was as if God hit him like the wall that came crashing down. He very nearly launched backward, surprising all of us with his abrupt descent to the floor. I continued telling him what I was seeing as it unfolded, not so much praying as reporting. I told him that God would "give His angels charge over him, to bear him up, lest he dash his foot against a stone." At this he burst into an uproarious laughter that nearly split blood vessels! The change in him was so dramatic that I began laughing, as well. He managed to say, "You have no idea what you've said, have you? You've no idea!" He then rolled about in fits of laughter again. I moved on to the next person, since I guessed that the Lord had touched him—I don't know, just a feeling I had.

The picture of what I had been shown remained

clearly with me, which was unusual. Almost a year later, I can still see much of what unfolded. It's somehow different now, as though changes have been made in it, as if it has been developing in a parallel world.

I can in no way corroborate my testimony. What I can offer is what all this meant to the vicar. In conversation with him later, I learned that each of the images I detailed for him exactly mirrored an event in his church. For instance, he had just recently supervised the demolition of a structurally unsound Anglican church, one that was built in the Middle Ages. In the process, he had tripped over a stone in that church, fallen, and received a head injury that had disabled him for over a year. He had also endured great spiritual opposition to his godly leadership, and was wondering if there was any hope in sight. Other details were prophetic or allegorical, and were profoundly encouraging to him.

While he was down on the floor, and quite apart from anything I had said to him, he had a marvellous experience of God's presence, in which the Lord truly apprehended him as his loving Father. The Lord ministered things to him in deeply personal and private ways, and when he rose from the carpet he was a new man. Out of my subsequent conversations with this vicar, I learned that because of what I had shared with him, he sensed that God was taking up residence in his parish, and that their congregation would figure significantly in this move of God. (This has indeed proven to be the case.)

The full story of this ministry time has many other twists and turns, involving dream sequences, middle-of-the-night phone calls, and things that go bump in the night. The vicar and his wife have since become some of our dearest friends, and God alone knows what is in store for them in the future.

I share these stories to illustrate that there is no formula for interceding in the Spirit. You simply have to speak out what you believe are God's thoughts and words. If you agree with Him and bless what He is doing, things may well get bizarre, but then, if so they will be a good kind of bizarre. Besides, who are we to define what is normal, anyway?

It's been a stretch. There is the sense that by times, revelations are thrust upon me. I have spoken what I thought were "visions" or "words," only to discover that my imagination was leaping up to the plate. I have received things that I thought were for the person I was praying for, but that applied to someone else, like the person next to them (go figure that one). I have looked, felt, and been totally humiliated in front of complete strangers (and survived) and I have worried needlessly about what others might think. One of the things I've realized is that people are not thinking about me as much as I think they are thinking about me. I have had to learn to live with much greater levels of uncertainty, and been pushed way outside my comfort zone, but the rewards have been wonderful.

In all of this, I have not checked my brains at the door; I *have* had to make changes in priorities. I now let my spirit lead my mind, and force my mind to serve my spirit. Given the revelations of God's love I have received, that is a perfectly rational thing to do; it is not yet habitual. I realize that I often will not know the complete picture, its impact or significance, but that this must not stand in the way of exercising the gift given. With great reluctance, I accept the fact that I will not be able to submit every vision, picture, feeling, etc., to the rigorous proofs required by science or the law. This no longer diminishes the veracity of those experiences. I continually live with ambiguity in signs, wonders, visions, and manifestations, having come to recognize that the outward phenomena are not always empirically declarative of the inner work of the Spirit, nor can one proceed to pray for people as if they were.

The best advice I have ever received on dealing with these issues is to "Love God with all my heart, strength, soul, and mind; and to love my neighbour as myself."

* * *

Jack Taylor, May 1995
Jack is a Southern Baptist pastor, who for the past twenty-three years has served as an itinerant speaker. He has authored twelve books, and has been an earnest student of revivals and awakenings. During his pastorate of seventeen years at the Castle Hills First Baptist Church of San Antonio, Texas, he experienced a wonderful reviving in the early seventies that resulted in hundreds of new

births and a church renewed, all of it accompanied by many unusual events. This reviving shaped many lives and still influences many people in many places. His first book, The Key to Triumphant Living, *chronicles this time of reviving in both personal testimonies and the corporate testimony of the church. When he and his wife, Barbara, heard of how God was moving in Toronto, they were immediately interested, and determined to observe what was going on as soon as possible.*

After reading about the renewal in the Airport Vineyard in *Time* magazine and other periodicals, we paid a visit in August of 1994. The meetings were then being held in the old facilities on Dixie Road. On our arrival, we were intrigued at all the people standing outside to get in. We waited in line to get into church for the first time in our lives on 23 August 1994.

The praises were inspiring, the sense of God's presence was clear, and the message, preached by someone other than the pastor, was pertinent, passionate, and pointed. Then came the ministry time, for which we were hardly prepared! (How could you be prepared for such with a traditional background?)

I had been in a period of "spiritual stretching" for years, ever since I had prayed that God would change my mind on every issue on which He and I did not see eye to eye. I had learned that much of what I thought was deep conviction was protectionism regarding cherished traditions. Thankfully, the strange series of manifestations at the Airport Vineyard did not repel me from the blessing I was to receive.

On the first night, prayer was offered for Christian workers, and both my wife and I went forward. As we were prayed for, we rested in the Spirit along with many others, and while in a prone position, I received physical healing and deep spiritual blessing. Both the healing and blessings have been completely confirmed in the months since.

One of those areas of confirmation is in the practice of prayer. I have always sought to maintain a disciplined prayer life. I have written a book on prayer, and have held many prayer retreats, prayer conferences, and prayer concerts. I have deep conviction that revival is born in prayer and borne on in prayer. What I experienced in Toronto in August of 1994 and during subsequent visits in December and in March of 1995 have further deepened that conviction.

What I sense of the Spirit's work at the Airport Vineyard intrigues me, for I believe that never before in the history of the church have so many people prayed for so many people. What I see is not a star-studded ministry of one ministering to many, but a powerful ministry of people praying for people. Since our first meetings in Toronto, I have been a part of this wonderful ministry "team," serving as I have throughout North America and England. I have had the double blessing of being prayed for and praying for people. This has touched and revised my prayer life in the following ways:

I pay more attention to listening to God for what to pray, rather than staying solely with a set prayer list. To my delight, I am finding that as I pray for people with an open heart to God, I can pray with His wisdom and not on the basis of my knowledge alone.

I am developing a mentality that dictates an optimistic outlook on problems. If God does indeed answer prayer, the worst of situations calls for concerted, believing prayer, with an expectation of an affirmative answer. I find myself more influenced by the promises of God than by the existence of the problems at hand. Anything is possible through prayer, because prayer links me to God, and anything is possible with God.

I am also discovering that the simple task of preaching is about praying for and exercising anointing (the enabling power of God) on the place of meeting, the period of time the meeting covers, the people who meet, the praises, the public prayers, the preaching, and the proposition that opens the ministry time. I am convinced that whether I am preaching to people or praying for them, what I am really doing is giving away the grace of God to them. Thus, my praying is receiving grace, living in grace, and giving away grace.

I am more conscious that I do not know how to pray, or what to pray for, and that the Holy Spirit is there in me and around me to orchestrate my praying. Sometimes it is in the form of silence and meditation; other times it is with words born of the Spirit, and still other times it is with "groanings which cannot be uttered." Though I still seek to maintain a time of prayer every day, I am more conscious through the day that the lines are open and there is pleasure in a consciousness that prayer really is the breath of the Spirit.

I continue to be impressed, not only with what happens in the lives of people prayed for in the meetings but with what happens in the lives of those who have committed themselves to pray for others. The awareness that I can give away the grace of God to needy people is a life-transforming concept. The fact that there are often manifestations when people are prayed for has added a fresh expectation to my praying. The "hereness" and "nowness" of the Spirit of God are factors that enhance the prayer life, whether personal and private, or public and corporate. Prayer takes God out of the "long ago" and introduces Him and His realm as our contemporaries. It is indeed as it is written in Hebrews 11:6: "He that comes to God must believe that He is, and that He is a rewarder of them that diligently seek Him." It seems to me that while many of the manifestations are strange and difficult to understand, the fact remains that God is using them to make the experience of His presence more real.

* * *

The bottom line as far as my own life is concerned is that as a result of this encounter with God, my passion for Christ is clearer, my own soul-peace more pronounced, and my own prayer life more consistent than ever. My love for the Scriptures, which has always been deep, has yet deepened more, and with it a concern for the world at large continues to grow. Added to all of this is an increasing awareness that I am part of the whole, exciting Body of Christ that has its members right round the globe.

I am also reminded of a story of a little girl in her church mission study who was encouraged to write foreign missionaries to inform them that she was praying for them. At the same time she was urged to let them know that they had no obligation to send her a written reply. Her letter was brief and to the point: "Dear Missionaries, we are praying for you ... we do not expect an answer." I have suffered from that expectation-less malady too many times. But now, as I see what is happening as a result of people praying for people, faith and hope are stirred, and I am more expectant of an answer.

I believe that we can expect the following results as these conditions continue:

1. Individual believers will find their spiritual lives rising to the level of their praying.
2. Churches will find their level of spiritual life rising to the level of the prayer lives of their individual members.
3. Individual believers will find their own prayer lives growing as they pray for others and thus discover a rising tide of spiritual power and authority.

4. As the practice of prayer is enhanced with the belief that it is an exercise that brings both immediate and long-range results, a higher view of prayer will give way to a higher practice and quality of prayer.

5. With dramatic answers to prayer exercised in an anointed atmosphere, there will come greater praise, which always results in still greater prayer.

6. New believers will learn to pray in this atmosphere generated by the Holy Spirit, and they will become radical and militant disciples of our Lord.

7. The renewal will mature through its baby stages, baby sounds, and baby ways to its full growth, and we may well expect the greatest harvest ever reaped in the history of the Church.

* * *

Loraine Daly, May 1995
Loraine is assistant to Steve Penny, senior pastor of an Assemblies of God church, the Christian Growth Centre, Sydney, Australia. She leads and trains their power team, and oversees women's ministries.

In mid 1994, our church began to hear of the world-wide move of God that has come to be known as the "Toronto Blessing." We heard of Aussie ministers who had gone all the way to Toronto to wait outside a church for two hours to get into the meetings! They returned full of the Holy Spirit and with fresh fire from Heaven. As a church, we began to seek renewal in our lives and church, and in October 1994, we held a week of prayer and fasting.

This time was to be a turning point in our church. Every night we gathered together to seek God. Pastor Steve Penny, our senior minister, said to us, "Mark this week down in your diary as the week that changed our church." God began to move powerfully in the prayer meetings, and many people received a gracious touch from the Lord. Every evening we set aside time to pray together corporately. One night God spoke to my heart and said, "You will set aside your heart for an hour for Me to come here and pray, but will you set aside your heart for the rest of your life, so you will never be the same again?"

I wanted as much as God would give me! Every time there was prayer being offered, I was the first one out to the altar and the last one to leave. As I lay before the Lord, I always prayed, "Lord, do your *whole* work tonight. I don't want to get up till You have done everything You want to do here. Lord, I want to get up different from what I was when I walked in here tonight. I surrender to you, Lord." I spent more time on the carpet than I did on my feet. All I wanted was the fullness of God's outpouring. The Bible says, "Eye has not seen, or ear heard the things God has prepared for those who love Him," and I began to feel God encouraging me that He had far more for us than I had anticipated.

The next month, Pastor Steve and his wife, Marion, took a team to Toronto to the prophetic ministry school conference that took place in November 1994. Before he left, Pastor Steve had been speaking about entering into the river of God. God spoke to me about going to Toronto and said, "If you jump off the bank and into the river of God here, you'll never be the same again. You'll never stand on this bank again. I'll take you further." I had to make the choice to move on into the river of God or stay where I was.

I earnestly wanted to go myself, but didn't know how I'd get there. The other question was "Do I need to go? If God's Spirit is moving all over the world, why do I need to sit on a plane for twenty hours??" I began to read the story of how Solomon was visited by the Queen of Sheba and many other kings from around the world, because God had given him something they wanted to get hold of themselves. That clinched it, and by God's miraculous provision, I was able to fly out to Toronto myself the following week.

For a number of years, God had been giving me a vision of what He had in store for me, through various prophetic words, as well as the witness of His Spirit speaking into my heart, but I had not yet seen any of it come to pass. Like Mary, when the angel of the Lord appeared to her, I "pondered the words in my heart," knowing they were yet to be fulfilled. I also knew I was not yet equipped for what God was calling me to do, but I waited and tried to prepare my heart for what God was purposing.

*   *   *

As I did "carpet time" during the meetings, God began to work things out of my heart, and pour His Spirit back in. One night as I lay there, I felt things being lifted off. I have no idea what they were, but God did. The Bible says "He knows the secrets of our hearts," and He certainly dealt with the secrets of my heart that night. I got up feeling noticeably lighter and freer in my spirit. The more God took out, the more room it gave Him to pour His anointing into my life. Every night God poured a new measure of grace into my spirit.

I rang home on the Saturday to see how the team had gotten on since their return. (It was Sunday afternoon back home.) I spoke to our associate pastor, David Palmer, after the Sunday-morning meeting. He told me the glory of God had fallen on the meeting, and that the presence of God was so strong he could barely stand as he led the meeting. People were being visibly touched and the sensed presence of God's Spirit was increasing. Those who had been to Toronto prayed for the congregation, and the blessing of God was being poured out most powerfully.

I hung up and phoned Pastor Steve in Singapore, only to discover that the meetings he was ministering at had become Holy Spirit meetings. He said that at times there was barely room to lay people under the presence of God. They were on stairs, on the platform, anywhere they could find space!

I then went off to the meeting at the Airport Vineyard, realizing that, at any given time, somewhere in the world, people were being graced by the Holy Spirit.

When I left for Australia at the end of the week, I prayed that this would not be the end of the outpouring of His Spirit, but the beginning of a new chapter in my life. I didn't want this week to become just a nice memory, but rather that God would continue to build on the work He had begun.

The Lord has honoured my prayer. Soon after my return, we began to hold meetings for anyone who just wanted to come and soak in God's presence. These soaker services were held midweek, and many people have come from all over Sydney and beyond to receive. At one of the meetings, I ran into a friend whom I hadn't seen for some time. She and her husband pastor a church out of Sydney, so I hadn't been in contact with them for a while, and she had no idea what I had been up to, or "down to," what with all of my "carpet time" both in Toronto and here in Australia. When she saw me, she kept looking at me, and finally said, "Loraine, you look terrific! What's happened?" I explained to her briefly what God had been doing in my life. She said, "As soon as I saw you, I knew something was different. You look like the person you were meant to be."

* * *

One thing I have discovered about this move of the Spirit is that it's more than just a wonderful revelation of the presence of God; it's also equipping for His service. I've learned this first-hand, because after my return from Toronto, Pastor Steve asked me to train what we call our power team, those who minister at the altar. This turned out to be timely, because in March 1995 we held a Spreading the Fire conference and invited Guy and Janis Chevreau and Larry Randolph to be our keynote speakers. People came from all over Australia and beyond, and God poured out His Spirit upon hungry souls all week. The power team have had the privilege of being used by God to administer His blessings, blessings that have washed over us too, many, many times.

At times the congregation swelled to 1,200 and beyond. We didn't have space enough. Ministry spilled over into two overflow rooms, and as I went from room to room to make sure there were enough power team members to pray, it was an experience I will never forget: in one room, there was a beautiful, gentle presence of the Lord, like rain falling from heaven, with people laid out, resting quietly before the Lord. I moved to the next room. There, uproar! Even the catchers were falling over laughing as they attempted to minister! There was no one standing in the whole room!

In one of the morning sessions, Larry Randolph moved through those seeking prayer. People were lined up in the aisles, unable to get to the front of the church. Larry began to move up the left-hand aisle, praying for those who stood against the sides of the church. A few minutes later I looked in that direction again. People were literally stuck against the wall, unable to move under the power of God. Good idea. Wall ministry. No catchers needed.

The following morning Guy Chevreau spoke, and following the second session we continued into a soaker service. Some stayed under the power of God or waited, still hungry for more. Others left for lunch, to return for the afternoon session. Those who had stayed were still being powerfully touched by God. Great waves of laughter swept through the room, until it seemed the whole building was laughing. As more people returned for the 2:00 P.M. session, they stood in amazement as they realized that what they were witnessing was *still* the soaker service from the morning meeting. I was told that they could hear the laughter as they crossed the road, to get back into the building! At 2:00 P.M. we carried people out into another room to continue to soak, so we could put the chairs back in and conduct the next session.

Testimonies of God's healing power have been coming into our office continuously since the conference. People tell of being healed of conditions they had lived with for years. People who were dry and literally going through the motions of their Christian life are now refreshed and on fire again for God. One lady wrote to us after the conference:

For us, the most exciting things are what is happening on the inside. A passion for Jesus, and a greater love for the body of believers. A greater desire to read the Word, which has come alive to us. We have noticed a greater release in the prophetic, with more visions and words. Thank you for investing so heavily in the Body of Christ; the fruit of this conference will be evidenced in the lives of many in this nation, to the glory of God. May He continue to bless you all.

We have continued to hold soaker services on Friday and Sunday nights. People are travelling up to three hours to be here and receive grace from the Lord, and the Lord's blessing has changed many people in our church.

For instance, a friend of mine had been abused in her childhood and raped during her teen years. This had left her withdrawn and mistrustful, and she has suffered from frequent bouts of depression and illness. Many times we prayed together for God to transform her life, and she has persevered despite the pain she felt inside. When we began to move in this outpouring of the Holy Spirit, she repeatedly came forward for prayer, and God has done a mighty work in her heart. She has been set free of fear and guilt over her past, and released from the pain of what had happened to her. She wrote to me recently and said, "As soon as I poured out my heart and let God take care of my problems, a weight lifted. I used to find it hard to see God as a loving Father—I never had a father figure as I grew up—but as I opened up and cried before the Lord, I now have confidence, and love towards other people; I'm not the scared person I once was. Times can be hard, but if you love the Lord and trust in Him, it doesn't seem so bad. I can now call the Lord my Dad, and He's always there when I need Him."

God *has* taken away my friend's pain and replaced it with His love and trust. She used to sit at the back of the church, ready to make a quick getaway should she start feeling uncomfortable, but now she's down at the front. Sometimes when she's sitting near me during the worship I can't help but peek at her. To see her standing and worshipping God in freedom, with love and trust in her heart, is evidence of the transforming power of God. Her face shines with the glory of the Lord as she worships her Heavenly Father.

This blessing is not just being restricted to the adults, either. Many of our children come forward to receive prayer. My friend's son, five-year-old James, came out for prayer one night. I prayed for him and he fell down under the power of God, lying completely still for about ten minutes. (If you knew James, you'd know that this in itself is a miracle!) When he got to his feet, I saw him standing there, holding his head with his hands and shaking his head, as though clearing his thoughts. I said to him, "James, did Jesus touch you tonight?"

"Yes," he replied. "When Jesus touched me, I felt funny all over!"

"What did it feel like?" I asked him.

"It felt like I could love God every day!" he told me excitedly.

James repeated this to his mother a few days later, when dressing for school. "You know, Mum, when you get that prayer at church, it makes you love God every day!" I thought later, that's really what it's doing for us all. It's making us love God every day.

In our church, a great unity among people has developed. People are being drawn closer together. As they move into a greater intimacy with God, they are becoming closer to each other. This is especially evident in our midweek home groups. People who previously stood back a little from others are now asking their group leader, "How can I get more involved with others in the group?" Staid, quiet people, now transformed by the power of God's love, are transforming their home groups as others see the evidence of the changes in their lives. As they begin to open up, others then start to share the deeper things of their hearts.

Marriages have also been touched. Many husbands and wives who were struggling relationally have experienced healing and a fresh love for each other. We are constantly hearing of couples rediscovering their love for each other.

Unsaved people are being touched by the presence of God, too, as people take the blessing out. I went out to dinner with a friend who was facing a crisis in her life. On the way over, I prayed the Lord would give her joy that night. We arrived at the restaurant and sat down, and all of a sudden, both of us began to laugh. The waiter had to come back three times to take our order, because we were unable to speak. The third time we pointed to the menu to indicate what we would like, because we still were having trouble speaking.

We continued to laugh through the entire meal. The waiter kept walking past us, trying to work out what we were doing. Eventually he came up to us and said, "I don't know what it is, but I've got it, too!" We watched him trying to pour coffee at the tables, his shoulders shaking as he tried to suppress the laughter. He then came and told us the chef was now laughing out in the kitchen. Two ladies sitting at the next table then began to laugh, sometimes with an expression of bewilderment on their faces as they tried to work out what they were laughing at!

We had the opportunity of sharing with the waiter later that night about God's Spirit touching people all over the world in this way.

* * *

As to how this outpouring of God's Spirit has affected people's personal prayer lives, the first thing of note is that there has been a significant breakthrough for so many. Personally, the Holy Spirit has much more pre-eminence in my life now. I used to have trouble praying by myself for any length of time, but now I find it so easy.

I pray at home before coming to our preservice prayer meeting, and on occasion, I am having such a great time at home in God's presence I think, "Do I have to leave this and go to a prayer meeting?" It reminds me that the same disciples to whom Jesus said, "Can you not watch with me one hour?" are the ones who, after being filled with the Holy Spirit, met constantly for prayer. It is now a continual joy to spend time with God.

There are other testimonies.

One power team member had an inability to deal with the stresses of her life such that she developed an internal condition, which required daily medication. Her doctor had also suggested she try Eastern meditation. As God poured out a fresh measure of grace in her life, she spent many hours saturating in His presence (truly meditating on God). As she waited on God, He showed her again and again that His ways are higher, so much higher than ours. As a result of the joy and peace God has placed in her life, she no longer needs her medication.

This same woman had prayed regularly with another lady for the past three years. Now they find they no longer use a list of prayer points. They quietly start praising Him, and then ask Him what He would have them pray for. Pictures or impressions come to them and together they join in prayer. They are seeing quick answers to prayer and God is at work in many lives that they have been praying for.

Another lady in our church has found since we moved into the blessing that the Lord is waking her every morning at five for prayer. God has given her a deep sense of His closeness, and with it a freedom to "see" in the Spirit. She sees spontaneous pictures of other people she is praying for, and when she shares them with those concerned, there comes release and blessing. For so many of us, God has made Ephesians 1:17–19 live:

> [May] the God of our Lord Jesus Christ, the all-glorious Father, confer on [us] a spirit of wisdom and vision, with the knowledge of Him that they bring ... , that the eyes of [our] hearts may be enlightened, so that [we] may know the hope to which He calls [us], how rich and glorious is the share He offers [us] among His people in [our] inheritance, and how vast are the resources of His power open to us who have faith.

Another of our power team members has been touched during her own prayer times at home. Initially she had not felt good about the laughter. It didn't sit with her image of God. But one night she began laughing, and when she got home she asked God to forgive her if she had offended Him. God continued to release within her a deep joy, and confirmed in His Word that this was from Him. After that there was no stopping her. God has released her from a background of abuse, as He has filled her with His Spirit to saturation point. The Lord has given her abundant joy and a passion to live, where for most of her life she wanted to die.

* * *

I have found that God has opened up a greater arena of spiritual awareness since He has touched my life. Many times when I pray for someone, I wait on the Lord, and He begins to lay upon my heart areas He wants to minister to in their life. We learned this from those on the renewal team from Toronto. I have found at times it is as if I begin to feel God's heart for a person, as I quietly wait before Him in prayer for them. I feel how God's heart is towards the broken-hearted and those who know their need. People who, on the outside, seem to have it all together; but when God puts a word in my heart and I share it, it unlocks a door for them and brings release.

This sometimes comes in some unusual ways. One night as I crouched over to pray for someone on the floor, I rested my hand gently on the top of her head. Then my hand turned over, so that the back of my hand was on the top of her head. I thought, "I didn't do that!" and turned my hand back to praying position number three, palm of hand on top of head. Again my hand flipped over. This happened about five times. Meanwhile I was quietly praying for the lady. I began to ask, "Lord, what are you trying to tell me?" Then I understood.

I bent over and whispered to her, "Pam, the Lord wants you to know His hand is not turned against you." I could see this was witnessing to her spirit. God started to show me more, and I continued,

"When you see the Lord's hand, it is not raised to strike you, but it is a hand of protection and provision to you." I continued to pray along these lines, being led by the Spirit.

Pam later shared with me that she and her husband were the only Christians on both sides of the family, and their family members had been giving them a really hard time about God and the church. She started to come under their condemnation, and even said to the Lord, "God, I feel like you want to smack me."

"Pam, the Lord wants you to know His hand is not turned against you."

What a gracious and loving Father we have!

CHAPTER SIX

LET YOUR GLORY FALL

Summary and Synthesis

Not by might nor by strength, but by my Spirit says the Lord of Hosts. (Zechariah 4:6)

* * *

In the delightful little book *Your Word Is Fire*, there is a story about a devout Jewish peasant. His attitude towards prayer is one of profound trust and faith in God's graciousness and goodness; this secure foundation is the very bedrock from which one intercedes in the Spirit.

There once was a simple man who used to address God in prayer and say: "Lord of the World! You know that I have not studied, that I cannot even read the holy words of Your prayer-book. All I remember of that which I learned as a child is the alphabet itself. But surely You, Lord, know all the words. So I will give you the letters of the alphabet, and You can form the words Yourself." And so, with great devotion he prayed, reciting the letters of the alphabet: *"Aleph, Bet, Gimel ..."* [1]

[1] Arthur Green and Barry Holtz, *Your Word Is Fire: The Hasidic Masters on Contemplative Prayer* (New York, Schocken Books, 1987) p. 9.

This current move of God's Spirit has called forth a radical humility from many, such that there is the recognition that in so many ways, we do ourselves a favour when we include ourselves among the "simple." In terms of prayer, the best we can do is offer to the Lord our heartfelt devotion, our groanings, our hope to see His will accomplished, and then attend to the "words" that He gives us as He takes the "letters" of our stammerings. By the power of His Spirit, He forms them into the Creative Word that calls forth life, within us and for others.

Through prophetic revelation, there comes more and more of Jesus, not only in us personally, but corporately, as His Body. The bishop of Lyon, Irenaeus, writing between A.D. 182 and 188, described the prophetic this way: "We hear many brethren in the Church, who possess prophetic gifts, and who through the Spirit speak all kinds of languages, and bring to light for the general benefit the hidden things of men, and declare the mysteries of God...."[2] Irenaeus brought these reflections to bear a full hundred and thirty years after the Apostle Paul wrote his first letter to the church at Thessalonica. There is, however, a strong pastoral continuity in the directives that Irenaeus and Paul call forth.

The Apostle's concluding admonitions in 1 Thessalonians 5:16–24 serve us as summary for our considerations as to what it means to pray in the

---

[2] Irenaeus, *Against Heresies*, V.6.1. Ante-Nicene Fathers, Vol. 1, ed. Alexander Roberts (Peabody Mass., Hendrickson Pub., 1994) p. 531b.

midst of this outpouring of God's Spirit. The context of these verses situates them as the conclusion of two important movements in the life of a young and actively charismatic church: the first is Paul's understanding of the ongoing impartation of the Spirit to believers—God *continues* to call them into His Kingdom and glory; the Lord *continues* to make their love increase and overflow; and God *continues* to bestow on them His Holy Spirit.[3] The second is that in the church at Thessalonica, there were some who were seemingly outstepping their prophetic authority. There were problematic declarations, particularly concerning resurrection and the second coming of Christ, and with such heavy future orientation, these carried some very unhealthy consequences. Misguided prophetic directives were causing some within the congregation to take liberties with their lifestyle; believers were passing judgements on each other and a spiritual elitism arose within the fellowship.

On a corrective basis, Paul calls the Thessalonian believers to *live* a life of joy and prayer, one that is rooted in gratitude, nurtures the Spirit's fire, and honours prophetic encouragement. Even though it's the prophetic that is the source of the problems in the church, Paul will not allow abuse to force disuse. Rather, what is required is discernment. They are to test the prophetic words brought forth.

[3] 1 Thessalonians 2:12 and 5:24; 3:12; 4:8.

So are we. On the last day of the Pentecost conference hosted by the Basileia Bern Vineyard in north-
east Switzerland, I had the privilege of teaching in the
morning plenary session. More than three thousand
had gathered for the conference, coming from all over
Europe. The Lord had graciously met with us, refreshing, reviving, and releasing more of His grace, as He
is doing all over the world. Later that day, it was time
to head back home. I preached from 1 Thessalonians
5:16–24, and in the course of the sermon conducted
an informal survey, asking the congregation, "How
many feel you've touched something more of God's
glory these past few days?" Many stood. "Had something of your emptiness filled? Your dryness refreshed?
The dullness awakened? Your vision sharpened? How
many have had your passion for the Kingdom
inflamed? How many have touched something more
of God's love, peace, and joy? Had something of fear
removed, despair, discouragement, anxiety lifted?"

It had been a great time together, so by the end of
the questions, nearly the whole congregation were on
their feet.

After we gave the Lord a praise offering, we went on
to recognize that it was not *pure God* we were seeing
manifested in the midst of the meetings. At any time,
in any place, the best that's demonstrated are our
physical, emotional responses to the experienced presence and power of God's Spirit. In that, it is always a
mixture of *flesh* and *Spirit*. That's why the Apostle
Paul admonishes that we are to "test everything."

What he doesn't spell out is how. As we find ourselves in the midst of this renewing, reviving, releasing move of God, it is imperative that we pray for
discernment, for wisdom and understanding, because
we must be continuously "testing the spirits," not to
find fault, to criticize, or condemn, but to intercede
for greater purity, greater anointing, and greater
Kingdom authority, such that the purposes of God
would find even greater fulfilment in our midst and in
our time.

To that end, it is helpful to distinguish revival and
revival*ism*. Iain Murray's work of that title is a careful
study of what he calls "The Making and Marring of
American Evangelicalism," and there is a tremendous
amount to be gleaned from his research, for many of
the dynamics that make and mar a work of God are
not so much tied to time or culture as they are to the
human spirit and soul.

* * *

Given even a little thought, we quickly realize that in
all revivals there are what previous generations called
"admixtures." What we live with is a mixture of flesh
and Spirit, at work in each of us. Regardless of how glorious the worship, how moving the testimonies, how
inspired the preaching, or how attentive the ministry, a
measure of our own "stuff" will always be mixed with
God's. In the heights of all that gets manifested in the
midst of this outpouring, it is our bodies, minds, and
spirits responding to what the Spirit of God is stirring

within us and calling forth. None of us ever makes a "perfect" response; things are yet tangled enough that there is always some measure of compromise, misdirection, even corruption. Lest this sound rather dismal, gloomy, and Eeyoreish, let it be underscored that at least in my experience, the balance of what's been experienced of the "Toronto Blessing" is the best I've ever seen, the closest I've ever come to what I understand Christian faith and Kingdom living to look like!

In our prayers for discernment, what we need to attend to are those things that are "eternally" called forth by the Spirit, and those things that move men and women only temporarily, that can be accounted for in psychosocial terms. The depth of zealous feeling demonstrated and the physical manifestations such as the falling and shaking, the laughing, and weeping, are not the means for distinguishing true spiritual awakening from momentary religious excitement. They are at best indicators, or signals, of a deeper, inner work.

As we proceed, it's helpful to consider what it is we understand and expect of revival. Murray defines things in very broad and simple terms: there is a larger giving of the Holy Spirit, and a heightened sense of His presence and influence. This is manifested, and thereafter recognized in others, by a new "degree of authority, warmth and joy that had not been there before." He says that "what characterizes a revival is not the employment of unusual or special means but rather the extraordinary degree of blessing attending the normal means of grace. There were no unusual evangelistic meetings, no special arrangements, no announcements of pending revivals."[4]

When two "streams" of American evangelicalism are contrasted, some critical distinctions arise, ones that are determinative for our understanding and practice of prayer. As a spiritual watershed, these two streams ultimately have different sources, and flow in opposite directions. If we give these two streams names, we would call one grace, the other works. The first is an open reception of gifts; the second, the exaltation of a methodology.

Murray says of the first:

No human endeavours can ensure or guarantee results. There is a sovereignty in all God's actions. He has never promised to bless *in proportion to* the activity of His people. Revivals are not brought about by the fulfilment of "conditions" any more than the conversion of a single individual is secured by any series of human actions. The "special seasons of mercy" are determined in heaven.[5]

In 1740, revival preacher Samuel Davies took up this very theme in a sermon titled *The Success of the Ministry of the Gospel, Owing to a Divine Influence*.

[4] Murray, pp. 107 and 129.
[5] Murray, p. 22.

The text for his message was 1 Corinthians 3:7: "So
then neither is he that planteth anything, neither he
that watereth; but God that giveth the increase." One
of his observations is particularly telling:

> The different success of the same means of grace,
> in different periods of the church, sufficiently
> shows the necessity of gracious influences to ren-
> der them efficacious ... it is not by power, nor by
> might, but by the Spirit of the Lord of Hosts that
> the interests of religion are carried on. Our own
> experience and observation furnish us with many
> instances in which this great truth has been
> exemplified.... We have seen persons struck to
> the heart with those doctrines which they had
> heard a hundred times without any effect.
> Whence could this difference arise, but from spe-
> cial grace?[6]

This account from the New England Prayer Revival of
1858 sounds a similar note:

> Awed by the manifest presence of God which we
> have felt to be around us, conscious that it has
> arisen from no measure of ours, nay, more that it
> has come in spite of our coldness, of our inac-
> tion, and of our indifference,—it is natural that

[6] Samuel Davies, *Sermons*, Vol. 3. (Philadelphia, Presbyterian Board
of Pub., 1864) pp. 24–27.

we should stand half-fearful, lest our hands should disturb, rather than advance the work— least of all presuming that we can direct its progress.[7]

The second stream flows in quite a different direction, originating, as it does, in different headwaters. Rather than attending to what God is doing, the focus shifts "from above," as it were, "to below," to what revival leaders themselves are orchestrating.

During the Second Great Awakening, for instance, the most common phenomenon that marked the revival was falling, "a temporary physical collapse." "People dropped as if shot dead, and they might lie, unable to rise, conscious, or unconscious, for an hour or for much longer. Some fell who had previously been sceptical of everything. Many—150, 250, even 800—were recorded as falling during camp meetings."[8] Without careful and prayerful discernment, there was the tendency to trophy the falling, shouting, sobbing, leaping, and swooning, as though such outward demonstrations were *necessarily* to be equated with inner conversion and transformation. These kinds of conclusions can be evidenced in nearly every revival in the past; it is, by times, the case today.

Murray is spot on when he states:

[7] "The Religious Awakening of 1858," in *The New Englander* (August 1858) p. 664, quoted in J. D. Hannah, "The Layman's Prayer Revival of 1858," in *Bibliotheca Sacra* (Jan–Mar, 1977) p. 71.
[8] Murray, p. 164.

The course of a revival, together with its purity and abiding fruit, is directly related to the manner in which such excitement [about physical manifestations] is handled by its leaders. Once the idea gains acceptance that the degree of the Spirit's work is to be measured by the strength of emotion, or that physical effects of any kind are proofs of God's action, then what is rightly called fanaticism is bound to follow. For those who embrace such beliefs will suppose that any check on emotion or on physical phenomena is tantamount to opposing the Holy Spirit.[9]

Functionally, revival*ism*, the second stream, is methodology, not mystery. Some, like Charles Finney, were so brazen as to assert that pastoral leadership was to be blamed if there was no revival, for he told his students:

Christians are as guilty for not having the Spirit, as sinners are for not repenting.... God has placed His Spirit at your disposal, and if you have not the Spirit, God has a right to look to you and to hold you responsible for all the good you might otherwise do.... You see why you have not a revival. It is only because you do not want one.[10]

[9] Murray, p. 163.
[10] Charles Finney, *Lectures on the Revivals of Religion* (London, Morgan and Scott, 1910) pp. 134 and 34.

Revivalism is so marked by the predictable that its promoters, past and present, are forward enough as to advertise beforehand that "revival" *will* take place. There is a strong expectation set that is developed, and with it a psychological pressure to conform; add to these the characteristically hyped personality of the centre-stage "revivalist," and one has very nearly guaranteed "success."[11]

* * *

Returning to 1 Thessalonians 5:21, and the admonition to "test the spirits," we are now further ahead than we were in terms of answering the question "How?" We now have other questions that help us discern: "What is the spirit of the meetings; how is the ministry conducted; and especially, what is the attitude taken in prayer?" Further, "Where, and in what ... and ultimately in *whom*, is confidence placed? Are things grounded in grace, or are they the fulfilment of a carefully strategized methodology? Is there a persuasive sense that all is rooted in the spontaneity of relationship, or is it more a matter of mastering techniques?"

Before we proceed, it is imperative to contrast judgementalism and discernment, for there is one key distinguishing dynamic that differentiates the two. What defines discernment and sets it apart from judgementalism is prayer. It works like this: judgementalism

[11] Murray, p. 380.

ultimately, and usually immediately, works against the Body of Christ; it whacks; it tears down; it divides. Discernment, however, seeks to build up the Body of Christ, to encourage and stimulate further good works. Judgement is fault finding; discernment is corrective. Much of this is subtly nuanced; the clincher comes in terms of prayer. Rule of thumb says: "If you're not interceding, you're judging. If, instead, you're praying for further revelation, speaking blessing, calling forth greater wisdom, and grace, and humility, there's a very good chance that you are bringing spiritual discernment to bear as you seek to build up and encourage the Body of Christ."

In terms of judging and discerning, it's also imperative for us to remember that each of us finds ourself somewhere on the continuum of Christlike character; what serves us most is if, instead of spending a great deal of time and energy discerning and testing *other* spirits in this deal, we instead concentrated on testing *our* spirits. For instance, is there a greater sense of gratitude up and out of what we've experienced? Has something in us been stirred, such that with new freedom, we are overwhelmed by God's goodness, and faithfulness, and generosity: do "Thank yous" quickly and easily fill our mouths? Or is there a new measure of pride at work ... "I've been to Toronto, and I got blessed"? Has a subtle elitism taken root: "If you were *really* hungry for God, you'd do whatever it takes to go to Toronto ... the way I did." Are there two types in the church, the "blessed" and the "blessed-nots"?

Humility and flamboyance can be contrasted. As we set out to worship, preach, or pray, are we asking continualy, "Jesus, I want the performer in me to sit down, You be the One standing up." In that, who is it we consider to be our audience? The assembled congregation or the Lord? Whose acceptance and approval are we seeking? As we test *our* spirits, are we seeking to give the anointing away, or show it off?

Pastors and leaders especially need to get it settled: is there a trustful abandonment to all that the Spirit calls forth, or are there dynamics of control at work? I've been in several churches where the host pastor wanted renewal to break out in his church, but as the various manifestations started to be evidenced, they outstretched the comfort zone. Sometimes a line would be drawn: "I won't have ... *that* in my church." The question needs to be answered: "*Whose* church is it?"

All of these dynamics are matters of the heart, and as such are subtly distinguished. We recognize only too quickly that the slide from godliness to carnality is an insidious and ever-so-slippery one. A final pair of contrasting "spirits" is especially provocative as some of us find ourselves nearing the second anniversary of this gracious move of God.

One can easily recognize the wonderful momentum that renewal and revival generates—the numbers of new people who keep on coming from all over; the conversions, the rededications, the restorations and the releases; the practical needs and concerns that hosting this move requires—in terms of facility, staff, and resources—the list is an extended one. With all that's happening, as quickly as it's happening, it is imperative that we test our spirits to discern if it is an *attentiveness* or a *presumptuousness* that motivates what we do.

It is so easy to presume. Given the demands, and the glorious problems that revival calls forth the new requirements on time and energy; the frequency of ongoing meetings; for leaders, the itinerant travel one quite innocently takes the anointing for granted, and relies on a previous sermon, or worship set, or established ministry guidelines. In the rush, we often find ourselves doing what worked before.

Consider the following as a parable. If the bio in the front of the book has been read, it will be recalled that when it's windy enough, I can be found windsurfing on Lake Ontario. That needs a bit of a qualifier, because I'm not always free to surf when the weather office issues the storm warnings. Lots of times I'm unable to cancel my appointments, and all that good wind goes to waste. I arrive at the beach the *next* day, only to discover that the wind is dying off.

If I try to sail, I know it will be a tremendous effort to stay afloat, because there's no speed, no board stability, and no way of determining any up- or downwind direction.

Because I missed it when it was "crankin'," I may try to go out in the "leftover winds," but conditions are really marginal. Often, I'll limp my way out a thousand metres and end up having to swim the rig back in, which is not fun at all.

As I struggle for shore, I'll usually mutter, "You can't surf yesterday's wind."

That saying serves well as we pray in the midst of this current outpouring of God's Spirit. We can't "surf" yesterday's "wind." Yesterday's anointing was for yesterday. What the Spirit revealed and released yesterday was for yesterday's ministry. Be it yesterday's music, yesterday's sermon, yesterday's prayer ... the anointing that was on it was for yesterday. What is before us is to attend to what the Lord is blessing and pouring out His Spirit on *today*. If we *presume* on past glories, and call them forward *today*, we'll find ourselves without any "speed," or "stability," or "direction." We may well end up way out of our depth, and have to swim for our lives.

*   *   *

Paul's instruction in 1 Thessalonians 5:16–24 names the inescapable tension that life in the Spirit calls forth: with both present revelation and all of the dynamisms released in the power of the Spirit, manifested in and through a gathered body of believers who are in the process of being sanctified, how does one nurture and attend to the graced vitality of all that the Spirit calls forth, and at the same time address the pastoral responsibilities of correcting, disciplining, even protecting a congregation from "charismatic abuse"? No easy answers will serve.

In the early months of the renewal, there was a free-dom, an abandon, even at times an extravagant liberty taken in the anointing that was being poured out. But as numbers have grown and the months have passed, there has come a recognized need to bring limits to bear, as to who prays for whom, and when, and how. Ministry team training and release, while essential, have also at the same time brought a measure of reserve, a stifling, at times even a quenching, of some of the Spirit's purposes; ever so insidiously, methodology sneaks in to take place over relationship.

The issue, however, is neither an unlimited and unfettered liberty, nor rules, regulations, and prohibitions. The heart of the matter is relationship—attending to "what the Father is doing." The call is clear. In John 17, Jesus prays for His disciples and those who will be raised up to follow. There are several themes intertwined throughout the prayer, themes of revelation, joy, glory, truth, mission, and together they weave a picture of perfect unity. Oneness. Intimate relationship.

> Father ... may they be one, as We are one.... May they all be one; as You, Father, are in Me, and I in You, so also may they be in Us.... The glory which You gave Me I have given to them, that they may be one, as We are one; I in them and You in Me, may they be perfectly one. The world will know that You sent Me, and that You loved them as You loved Me.[12]

[12] John 17:11; 21–23.

It is so very easy to lose the awareness of God's presence and immediate purpose in the urgency of the moment, even when that moment is ministry! We can so quickly rely on what we've learned, and practised, and seen blessed in the past, instead of attending to what the Lord has for us, what He wants to impart to us and through us, in the moment. In the attempts to conduct things decently and in order, it is so easy to outstep ourselves and introduce aspects of control that limit the Spirit, even grieve the work that He purposes, because of the new box we've fashioned for God—a "renewal" box. We're then back working out methodologies, seeking to master new techniques, and in so doing, we push away from grace, and the relational connection the Lord desires to have with us. Once again, works triumph over grace, and we're left living with the grim realities: "[f]lesh only gives birth to flesh; it is Spirit that gives birth to spirit."

The Lord's prayer for His Church is nothing less than oneness, an unbroken, uninterrupted intimacy, Heart to heart, Spirit to spirit, *with us*. As problems and difficulties arise, both personally and corporately, it's not *our* solutions and methodologies that are required; it is before us to intercede for the Spirit's direction and conviction, to ask for further revelation and for even greater freedom.

*   *   *

A final story, a picture worth a thousand words:

A father and his son were travelling together in a

wagon, when they came to the edge of a forest. The father pointed out some bushes, thick with berries. Excitedly the son asked, "May we stop so that I can pick some?" The father took pleasure in his child's enthusiasm and gladly brought the wagon to a halt. The son was soon enthralled with his newfound wealth.

After a while, the father wanted to continue on his way. But his son had become so engrossed in berry picking that he could not bring himself to leave the forest. "Son," called the father, "we cannot stay here all day! We must continue our journey. Come, back up beside me!"

But his pleas were not enough to lure the boy away. Surely he loved his son no less for his zeal, and he could not think of leaving him behind—but they really did have to move on, for there was so much more to their journey.

The father called out to his son, "You may pick your berries for a while longer, but be sure that I don't get too far ahead, for I shall start moving slowly along the road. As you work, call out, 'Father! Father!' every few minutes, and I shall answer you. As long as you can hear my voice, know that we are still close. But as soon as you can no longer hear my voice, know that you are lost; run with all your strength to find me!"[13]

In this season, God is graciously calling us to a greater relational connection than many of us have

[13] See Arthur Green and Barry Holtz's original story in *Your Word Is Fire*, p. 109.

ever known. From the Lord's generous hand, we are feasting with delight! But as we celebrate His goodness, we must be ruthless with the affections of our hearts, for it is very possible to become so engrossed in our "berry picking" that we fail to attend to the sound of His voice. If, in the excitement of the moment, we have done so, it is before us to repent, to confess that yet again we have become more enamoured with the gifts than we have been with the Giver.

What is called forth is faith; faith that He who calls has yet more with which to bless us. Stopping too soon dead-ends the Lord's leading; we must be assured that the Lord will ever call us on, not so much to a final destination, but to greater and greater intimacy, such that the prayer of Jesus is fulfilled: "The glory which You gave Me I have given to them, that they may be one, as We are one; I in them and You in Me, may they be perfectly one."

S.D.G.

SELECTED BIBLIOGRAPHY

Calvin, John. *The Institutes of the Christian Religion.* Trans. Ford Lewis Battles. Grand Rapids, Mich.: Eerdmans, 1975.

Cohen, J. M., trans. *The Life of Saint Teresa.* Edinburgh: Penguin Books, 1957.

Dunn, James D. G. *Jesus and the Spirit.* London: SCM Press, 1975.

Evans, Eifon. *The Welsh Revival of 1904.* Worcester: Evangelical Press of Wales, 1969.

Fee, Gordon. *God's Empowering Presence: The Holy Spirit in the Letters of Paul.* Peabody, Mass.: Hendrickson Pub., 1994.

Grudem, Wayne. *The Gift of Prophecy in the New Testament and Today.* Westchester, Ill.: Crossway Books, 1988.

Hannah, John. "The Layman's Prayer Revival of 1858," *Bibliotheca Sacra.* 134 (Jan-Mar 1977) 59–73.

McGee, Robert. *Search for Significance.* Houston: Rapha Pub., 1990.

Merton, Thomas. *Contemplative Prayer*. New York: Image Books, 1969.

Murray, Iain. *Revival and Revivalism: The Making and Marring of American Evangelicalism, 1750–1858*. Edinburgh: Banner of Truth Trust, 1994.

Weisberger, Bernard. *They Gathered at the River*. Boston: Little, Brown and Co., 1958.